Also, by Gary L. Eder

Children's books

Uncle Wrigley and the Snow Bush-A Christmas Story

Uncle Wrigley and Twigley the Flying
Squirrel's Candy and Cupcake Store

Uncle Wrigley visits the Easter Bunny
Web site: www.unclewrigleyvisitstheeasterbunny.com

A WINDOW OF OPPORTUNITY

KNOW WHEN TO KEEP TALKING AND KNOW WHEN TO START WALKING

GARY EDER

authorHOUSE®

AuthorHouse™
1663 Liberty Drive
Bloomington, IN 47403
www.authorhouse.com
Phone: 833-262-8899

Published by AuthorHouse 12/03/2020

ISBN: 978-1-7283-6888-7 (sc)
ISBN: 978-1-7283-6886-3 (hc)
ISBN: 978-1-7283-6887-0 (e)

Library of Congress Control Number: 2020914566

Definitions and other authoritative references in this book are for informational purposes only and are based solely on the author's experience. Also, any illustrations or photos are only examples of a subject to make a point. Due to the extensive time frame, many of those acknowledged or in recognition could not be contacted in spite of best faith efforts.

Print information available on the last page.

This book is printed on acid-free paper.

A Window of Opportunity

Seize it!

This book is a work of real-life experiences on the Art of Negotiations, and each "Short Story" is a factual accounting of actual events.

The other parts/chapters of the book concerning the Art of Negotiation$, from **consumer purchases of personal items to contract negotiations**, are solely based on the authors' experience and best practice recommendations.

For;

My wife, Karen, son Roy, daughter's Julie and Melanie

Our (8) grandchildren in seniority order; Roy III, Logan, Gloria, Eva, Ella, Evelyn, Landon, and Ethan. See below at the beach, also, for my two brothers William Irvin and Timothy Lee.

They're always there for each other, not their selves. Each a blessing
The elite 8, L-R, Logan, Ethan, Evelyn, Landon, Ella, Gloria, Eva, Roy III ☺
This picture by Melanie Pizzini December 2017

A special remembrance of my mother; Gloria Ann (Suze) Eder and my father William Leo (Bud) Eder

Picture from the mid-1970s. Bud and Suze were names of affection.

CONTENTS

EDITORIAL CREDITS

I'm thanking the following for their expertise in editorial corrections, subject photos, and information verifications. Their assistance was invaluable and much appreciated when you undertake writing such as this one.

Senior Editors:
Andrew Long III
Erik Decker

Editors:
Julie Ann-Marie Grove
Melanie Joy Pizzini
Milt Beever
Ralph Patinella
Doug Watley
Debra Moore Carter
George Gaye
Ava Eder

Illustrations/photo credit
Melanie Joy Pizzini
Roy L. Shover, Jr.
Rodmen Nelson
Timothy L Eder
John Gibson

INTEGRITY
Created by your actions

INTRODUCTION

First, let me say you'll be so pleased after reading this book and putting some of the learned negotiating skills to work, that you will have to go to a plastic surgeon to get the smile off your face.

So here I am now in my 73rd year of life (Hal le lu Jah) with over five decades of experience in the labor-management collective bargaining world (whew) along with various consumer negotiations on a personal level. As an author of several children's books, I decided to write about something more in line with my career. To write about what I have learned in the "Art of Negotiations." Also, to share some **"short stories"** that not only have direct meaning to this work but, in some cases, are amusing and downright funny.

I want this to be a learning experience for those who dedicate their working lives to collective bargaining and the administration of a contract. For the experienced that are interested in learning new ideas and the less skilled negotiators, the negotiators to be, **on both sides of the bargaining table, in labor-management negotiations.**

This writing is also for those in regular day to day life, for those at the consumer "bargaining" table involving buying a home, investments, your first car (new or used). How about those household updates; living room and bedroom furniture, a modern kitchen remodel, replacement windows, a new roof. When coming upon a circumstance that requires negotiating, some part of this book may save you some $$$ money!

The first part of the book discusses my
qualifications for writing this book.
The balance of the book has some real-life
experiences on the Art of Negotiations.

Believe this, if you don't believe anything else, the stronger your opponent, the more enhanced you'll become in your skill level. If you have shot pool are playing cards, scrabble, checkers, chess, or something more physical, like dancing, swimming, wrestling, bowling or playing soccer, etc., against superior players, you'll find your play level will elevate accordingly. That's what will happen to your negotiating skills.

At some point in your life, there may be a better negotiator across the table. But what this book is all about, is for *YOU to be the better negotiator.* It is for you to excel in the area of negotiating. Whether it's the car that you just bargained for, a house, or multi-million-dollar labor-management negotiations that you may have lead or been a participant.

So, how do you become an experienced negotiator? Well, first, listen, and observe. (see pages 43,44) Use what you feel would best fit your style and your personality. You cannot mirror someone else, no matter how experienced they are. You are your person, learn and recognize your skill level, and, more importantly, accept your area of weakness. Once realized, try to strengthen it. Don't be ashamed to admit your fault. Admitting a weakness to others can be a strength, and by doing so will show strength in your character.

Most importantly relax, it shows your confidence. Enjoy the negotiation you are in, and be thankful for the opportunity. When you succeed (not if), use those skills for the next opportunity.

I always wanted to be the best I could be in whatever game or position. e.g., *(Twenty-eight years*, from first-line union representative to successfully higher positions on the Union's Executive Board to Union President to National Vice President) **without a loss!**

And, *Fifteen years* as a Commissioner of Mediation, receiving numerous performance awards, by handling high profile cases. Now an Arbitrator with a successful arbitration practice and an established Author. When you put the desire and effort, it takes to add to your skill level and strengthen your weaknesses, and you will excel in your chosen field.

Another point that I always shared when training in contract language or advanced contract training negotiations and labor management training was to tell the group what to avoid. I wanted to let the class or individual know what NOT TO DO! **What to avoid** (page-75) The goal is always to improve your bargaining skills and, hey, maybe along the way, share with someone else the skills you learned and obstacles you avoided and how you did it.

I can't say enough about the need for preparation, no matter what you're negotiating. Do the research necessary depending on the issue. If it's a labor contract negotiation, check the number of employees and their seniority in 5-year increments, review the cost associated with each proposal, for the Union; take surveys of the membership, and if the employer, check with mid-level managers wants and list them in priority order. Marry those with the various contractual language proposals created. Weigh them based on importance and value (both economic and strength of language) before sitting down at the bargaining table, understand what your leverage is, or isn't! Don't Be *Rushed!*

If it's an automobile, do comparison shopping, get the car facts/history. Have this information at your side when you start bargaining. If a new car, ask if you still get the rebate along with the 0% interest financing? If they offer both, shouldn't you get both!? Know your credit rating in advance. There are (3) credit bureaus; Experian, Equifax, and Transunion. It can take some effort, but it pays off. As now, you have your rating for anything else you are purchasing. The dealer is not going to let someone walk away, who has a high credit rating (730-800+). Why? Because they know that a person/couple will not be delinquent on any payments. So, use that as a bargaining chip.

If it's a new suit or home furnishings, there is always something to add to the negotiations. The new suit, tell the sales clerk, you love it but would feel better about the price if something else like a reduced cost on a tie, ascot, belt, suspenders, or even IF YOU PUSH, a reduced rate on a shirt? Remember, you have to be ready to "start walking!" The last time I checked, there was more than one clothier, furniture store, etc. If you're able to get something else, consider it a win.

If it's living room furniture, how about negotiating a deal on a picture that the furniture stores hang purposely by a living room set that makes it look great over the sofa, or a side chair and lamp! **Remember, you can not show any expression of desire or want.** Try it; you'll have fun and save some $$$. Especially IF you can buy an item with cash, and if you can, use that as **leverage.** You'll see how fast the negotiations go in your favor.

Oh, hey, how about buying that home? Again this is where your credit rating comes into serious play that you already checked out, RIGHT?. Whether it is a car, suit, furniture, or home, you are in the driver's seat!

CHAPTER ONE
(First Failed Negotiations)

At age 14 (1961), this is when you think that you're smarter than your parents. Usually, it's much later in life that you discover that your parents have always been more intelligent, as it just took you a while to find out. But for me, I learned that at age 14. Having been blessed with a full crop of thick black hair, compliments of my mother, it wasn't unusual to find me in our singular bathroom primping.

It was an early September fall morning. The second week of school now in the 8TH grade. It was an especially great morning and too beautiful of a day to be going to school. So not knowing my limitations at that age, I decided to outwit my mother. It just so happened that the school bus stop was right in front of our home. I didn't have to walk far in the rain or the cold snow, only about 20 yards (twenty steps). So, I decided to miss the school bus and stayed in the bathroom, waiting to hear the bus to pull off. I ran out of the bathroom with a look of "aw shucks," I missed the bus! Mother standing in the kitchen, gave me the "you think I don't know" look and then said, "Well, Mr., you'll just have to walk to school!" Now the school was about a (5) five-mile walk. "But Mom, I'll be late anyway, and it's a long walk, so why not stay home? Also, I don't think that there is any test today." She replied, "You should have thought of that while waiting in the bathroom. Now off to school."

So off I went walking to school, a lesson learned, and a failed negotiation. That was missing what? **"Preparation, leverage, and no thought as to the worst-case scenario."** I'm smiling now as I write this, but felt kind of dumb as I walked to school, kicking stones along the way. You know what, the bus ride would've been a lot better!

Of course, this is not me back in 1961, so I asked a grandson to fill in.

The year 1961, No. 1 song. "Tossin' and Turnin', which I'm sure I did a lot of that night!"

CHAPTER TWO
Lesson Learned-When to Start Walking!

Age 15, the lessons learned at this young age are priceless, as you'll learn in relationship to actual negotiations, is to be *prepared, know the consequences, be ready for a worst-case scenario.* My childhood was a great one. A fantastic father and loving mother, so very lucky and fortunate for me and my brothers Bill and Tim. Our father was the enforcer and our mother, the protector. When there was an issue at school, it was a mom who came to protect. Always knowing (as I'm sure she did) that dad was there if needed.

One day mom sent me to get a pound of ground beef from our country store grocery. When I brought it home, there was a Blowfly in the meat! She immediately told me to return the ground beef and get the $$ back. When I went to return it, the grocer offered another pound of ground beef. I said, "no, thanks, just give me the money back." The grocery argued, "Hey, this is good meat, so tell your mother." I felt like saying, "you tell my mother," but I wasn't that cocky...yet! Mother was always quick to return wrong items; food or clothes, it didn't matter. She was teaching me the art of negotiations, maybe without really realizing it? No, I'm sure she understood the specialized training that was being shared, even-though not in a school setting. Her expertise was to know when to start walking. Again, I said to the grocer "no thanks" and started walking—*the top song that year; The TWIST.* I'm sure the grocer was in a *Twist* as he was left with soiled meat as *I walked out the door with the money!*

A skill I took in every consumer purchase and throughout my collective bargaining career.

CHAPTER THREE
U.S. Navy Vietnam Era

Upon graduation from high school, the draft was in full swing during the Vietnam War, and I was fortunate to have a selection in joining the Marines, Army, Air Force, Navy, or one of the associated reserve units.

The MARINES!! Our father, William Leo Eder Jr., was a MARINE and held to the saying, "Once a Marine always a Marine." Dad enlisted early at the age of 17 in 1933 and needed a signature to be accepted. He was stationed on the U.S.S. New York Battle Ship for the next 48 months, mostly at sea! **The top song that year," Stormy Weather,"** which I am sure they had a lot. The ship named after, New York, was probably the reason he was always a damn Yankee fan. Onboard, he was part of an 80 Marine detachment, mostly at sea, and even though the ship was named after New York, causing his love for those Yankees. It also gave him a lifetime dislike for water! So, no cruises in Dad's life. That helped me decide against the Marines, but dad had said that the Navy had the best food!.

The ARMY; My older brother William Irvin Eder drafted in 1963 following the Korean war. He waited for the draft as he was "making too much money to enlist." Always good in finances, he went from around $400 a month to 72.86 dollars a month in the Army. So, he was right about losing money and felt they were "miserable s.o.b.s" to demonstrate that, by coincidence, a **Top song that year was "The End of the World.**

To my brother who loved $$$, I'm sure it was. Anyway, that helped me decide against the ARMY. For those reading this who don't understand that comment on how he felt, just know that when you're in the military, IT IS NOT A DEMOCRACY, you do what you're told when you're told, as *there* IS NO voting! In those years, if you didn't report back from leave on time, the M.P.s (Military Police) would come and get you! What a change in times, huh?

The Airforce; no one in our family held that legacy. So my decision was made mostly on wits. I wasn't smart enough to be accepted and yet smart enough to know that, and therefore avoided rejection.

The NAVY; here I go. I registered for the draft immediately upon graduating from High School, applied for the U.S. Navy, was accepted that same June. A year later went on active duty on May 15th, 1966. **A Top song that year, "Reach out, I'll be there."**

It was a two by six program, two years of active duty, and four years of active reserve duty. My tour of active duty was in the Atlantic Theater, our task to monitor Soviet submarines, track and record their position, as this was in the so-called "cold war era." In addition to the Vietnam War being in full conflict.

It was a pretty good duty stationed on a Destroyer, the U.S.S. Charles H. Roan, DD 853. The balance of the tour was mostly in the North Atlantic, having stopped in Rhodes Greece, Ibiza, Rota, and Barcelona, Spain, Malta, plus Italy. Again, like my father, after being on this "Tin Can" in very rough (very rough) seas, there was absolutely no future cruise after this mandatory one. Especially since you have to PAY for those, pay to get seasick? No thanks. No matter how good the food is!

Now looking back, the experience of the military was not only rewarding but gave you a sense of pride and patriotism. It also gives you overall respect for the military as a whole. You are gone away from family for several months or a year at a time. During this time, you're making friends and experiencing parts of the world most people will never see and all at the expense of the U.S.A. Would I do it again?

YES!

Here we are entering the harbor at Malta in the Mediterranean Sea, 1968-1969 time frame. I was standing amidship (middle) facing the port side (left) with fellow sailors at attention with white helmets. Behind us was the Asrock Missle Launcher. A Top Ten song in 1968, **"Sitting on the Dock of the Bay."**☺

Oh, by the way, I stand for the National Anthem and have proudly displayed our American Flag on every home I have lived in.

Photo taken courtesy of the U.S. NAVY

CHAPTER FOUR
Employment-skill development

June 15th, 1965 and fresh out of school, 18 yrs. Old, A **Top song** **"(HELP)."** *I need somebody,* and I did get *help,* see below. A job at Westinghouse...wow a real job Starting at $60.85 a week as a labor grade (2) two mail clerk (there wasn't a labor grade one). A dream come true. There is truth to the saying, "it's not what you know, but who you know." **My Aunt Thelma** was a professional secretary in the Human Resources department at the (Circle Bar W), an acronym for Westinghouse Electric Corporation. She**, "Helped,"** get my first start in employment. God bless her; she was my father's youngest sister, who left us too early.

My first part-time job a couple of years earlier was a Soda Jerk at Dairy Queen (now called a "crew member"), I believe. I was making about $30.00 a week with no pension or medical benefits. Now, at Westinghouse, I doubled that amount and, although not understanding the benefits of receiving Health insurance, a Pension, and a 401k savings account. And at age 18, it didn't seem important, but it was! I was just too young to realize this tremendous benefit. *Benefits negotiated in a labor contract* with Westinghouse Electric Corporation and the Union; Salaried Employees Association, to which I (joined upon being hired) and later became not only it's Union President but one of its five National Union Vice Presidents.

On May 15^{th,} 1966, I did my active duty deployment and received an Honorable discharge in May 1972, returned to Westinghouse after active duty. **No. 1 song, "The First Time Ever I saw Your Face."** Is what I'm sure many people were saying when I returned to work, as I was on active military leave for that time frame. It was at Westinghouse where I developed the A and B of negotiations. A. "Your Word," when you give it, keep it and B. In maintaining your word, you are developing the B, "INTEGRITY."

In my early career, a handshake would follow anything you verbally negotiated. I have never had any remorse as a result of a handshake. Lucky? Maybe or just integrity on both sides. It does make a difference if you are negotiating something for only yourself versus someone else, a group, your employer or a bargaining unit, etc. **In these latter circumstances, a written contract, documenting language, and respective agreement is necessary.**

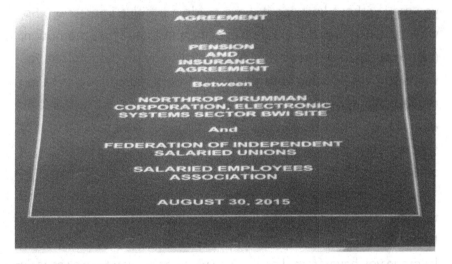

Past union contract.

Self-development

Can you bargain as an employee with your employer, company, agency, etc.? Sounds undoable, right? Here's how, if at the **"beginning,"** you always try to do your best. Excel at your assignments, build yourself a reputation as someone who is at work each day, on time, a self-starter who needs little or no direction, then you may without knowing it, have made a positive impression. So, when applying for a new position or being considered for a promotion, (your *reputation proceeds you.*) Then bargaining on the job that you want, you are bringing with you a good work record. You can then request $$$ as you're in a much better position to get it. Don't be afraid to ask for more money or something else, like a parking spot or special hours of work. So, you see, there is room for negotiations in almost everything.

If you develop these attributes, you'll be known for them, and they will drive your life in a positive direction, and you'll be so much better for it. Think about it. Through preparation, you'll find out what leverage you have; from that, you can plan on the worst-case scenario and be prepared to win at your negotiations. Be persistent in your demands or position. Again, don't *forget *common sense,* weigh that with your needs so you'll know when to walk.

*I understand that in some academic circles, common sense is referred to as: "the lowest form of intelligence." You know what, the use of common sense has probably settled more disputes than we can collectively count.

CHAPTER FIVE

(No Good Deed Goes Unpunished)

In 1974 as a relatively new union representative, representing at the time about eight different classifications (page 113) crossing over about 75 employees. **A Top 10 song that year, "Bennie And The Jets."** As a new representative, I felt like "Bennie."

As a union representative, I filed a grievance on behalf of an employee who had received a written warning of a potential suspension for continued missed time (absenteeism.) Previously the employee had already received a verbal warning, which is the first step of progressive discipline procedure in the Collective Bargaining Agreement (C.B.A.) (page 112) between Westinghouse Electric Corporation and The Salaried Employees Association, my local.

The grievance procedure of the contract called for a (3) step grievance procedure. Accordingly, I set up a step (1) meeting with the Human Resources manager to get an agreement to remove the disciplinary "written warning" action. The result follows:

The meeting resulted in this; If the grievant doesn't miss any time in the ensuing month, then the written warning would be rescinded and record expunged. **However,** (a word that became a favorite of mine over the next 45 years.) Along with, **but!**) But, (here it is) if the grievant missed any time the letter would stay, the grievant would move to the next step of the progressive disciplinary procedure, a (3) three-day disciplinary suspension without pay.

Now I argued, "how about some leeway. Suppose the grievant has an accident on the way to work or is in the hospital? Come on; I negotiated; give me something less severe." Now the H.R. manager said ok. "I'll give the grievant the benefit of the doubt if no more than three occurrences in the ensuing month. I'll rescind the written warning."

A handshake followed, and off I went to give the grievant the great news.

Later that day out on the manufacturing floor, I met with the grievant and gave the good news. I was shouted at and told that agreement was an impossibility and that there was no way not to miss time in a month! I explained you only have to make it work for about (20) twenty days, not 30 as the weekends don't count! But to no avail, it didn't matter; the grievant walked away unhappy. I had to chalk that up to "no good deed goes unpunished" I went on to other duties.

One month later

So, a little over a month later, I was called back into the H.R. manager's office, at which time I was showed the attendance record of the grievant, that recorded (6) six absences in the Month time frame. He said that the disciplinary procedure would move to the next step of (3) three-day suspension. I understood and went back to my duties as a Material Coordinator and Union representative.

Six years later

Now recently elected as a Union Executive Board member (1980), I had several occasions to represent employees while handling over 45 classifications of around One Thousand Five Hundred employees. One afternoon, after leaving a grievance hearing, the same H.R. manager (from the case above) pulled me aside and said the following; "Do you remember the time concerning the attendance case and the one-month agreement?" I replied, yes. Well, he said, "that was the point in which you built your integrity with me." As he went on, "you didn't come whining back when the employee missed more than the allotted absences. You used common sense and knew the employee received a fair agreement. You reached out your hand, shook hands, made an agreement, and KEPT it." **A top hit in 1980, "Another Brick in The Wall."** Kind of fitting, eh.!

Integrity Built

I didn't know what reputation I was developing. I couldn't because I wasn't in the higher-level management meetings, but apparently, the word went around that I was a Union representative with who you could reach an agreement. None of us know what reputation we are creating, but I can't stress enough that living up to an agreement that you either signed or shook hands-on is so.... Critical, and I guess you could say I built MY credibility and integrity, "brick by brick."

Lesson: Integrity established.

CHAPTER SIX
Your Word

Westinghouse Electric Corporation was the perfect environment to develop the Art of Negotiations. It was a corporate giant in those days and had facilities all over the U.S.A., and most of these had a Union organization. I was hired at the facility in Linthicum, MD. It was located by the then; Friendship International Airport, later to become the Thurgood Marshall Baltimore Washington, International Airport.

There were (3) Unions located there; The International Brotherhood of Electrical Workers, (I.B.E.W. Local 1805) The International Union of Electronic, Electrical, Technical, Salaried, Machine and Furniture Workers, later to merge with the Communication Workers of America, (IUE-CWA-Local 130) and my local Union; The Salaried Employees Association, (S.E.A.), affiliated with the Federation of Independent Salaried Unions. (F.I.S.U.)

A. B. C.'s of negotiations, learned at an early age, later expanded on as a Union representative.

A. **YOUR WORD** (*giving your word* and **KEEPING IT!**) develops integrity
B. **INTEGRITY** (*honesty* develops **TRUST**)
C. **LEVERAGE** (preparation, knowledge, worst-case scenario=RESULTS)

Don't forget: Common sense

An old saying that I like to refer to and used when teaching Collective Bargaining and Contract Interpretation courses is..."*If you can look in the mirror at the end of the day and know you were honest, did the best with what you had to work with, then you did right, go home and feel good about yourself.*"

Your word is the foundation on which you build on, then develops the **integrity** for what you are known. Now I want to expand a little further in the next chapter and take a look at some negotiation definitions that solidify the art of negotiation.

CHAPTER SEVEN
Definitions For grievance handling

Time frames; In the grievance and arbitration sections of the parties' collective bargaining agreements, there are usually specific time frames for filing, meeting, answering, and advancing unresolved grievances. And, for filing arbitration requests. Pay attention to the time frames specified. Develop a contract interpretation course and make sure that the time frames are part of it, maybe in a quiz format. As missing a time limit in the course of a grievance-arbitration process could make a substantial issue a mute one.

In-fact missing a time frame could make the issue a case of arbitrability. Most **procedural arbitrability** arguments fall under time limit disputes. It's essential to become knowledgeable about the contract that you are negotiating.

Why? Well, you want to win, don't you? Remember C. in the A.B.C.'s *preparation, knowledge,* it includes having a working knowledge of the contract you are challenging, amending, bargaining.

In the next chapter on continuity explains why it's essential to have a chain of experience and knowledge in both labor and management ranks.

CHAPTER EIGHT
Continuity

The parties to a collective bargaining agreement should and often do, set up a training program after the signing/ratification of the contract. I would also suggest that each party should also develop a more specific contract training course, and develop a test or quiz, issue a certificate of accomplishment for successful completion. Why? Because in both the labor and management world of negotiations, you want to have a solid base of contract knowledge. It helps the administration of the C.B.A. move more fluently. It helps maintain the continuity upon the transition from one Human Resource manager to another and one Union leader to another. Otherwise, there can be a loss of the intent of previously negotiated contract language and, therefore, loss of the meaning!

Example
Here's a great example of the loss of continuity; the parties negotiated a new language in the Sick leave Article of the C.B.A. They were moving the allotted number of sick days from 6 annually to 2 per quarter. The quid pro quo; (give and take), was now the employee taking a sick day cannot work overtime the day after using a sick leave day. There was no relative language written. But it was the intent and agreement of the parties at the table at that time. So, in the change of the lead negotiators, the purpose of the unwritten language is lost, as is the quid pro quo! Get it? Thus, the parties must now look at the practice, dig out the usage of sick days, and recorded O/T not taken as a result. To resurrect the agreement. Not easy!

Where in, if the reporting line to the leadership was trained and aware.

Then referring to memory would not be needed, and the agreement under the Sick Leave article not lost.

This example is just a minor circumstance of the loss of continuity. Expand on it, and you can readily see how critical it is to have a solid "trained base" for **both labor and management** to continue a strong bargaining history. A trained base keeps you from losing the knowledge of where you were or where you're going!

Example of *loss of continuity, due to **lack of trained** base. Illustration by Timothy L. Eder November 9, 2019.*

CHAPTER NINE
The (3) Sectors of Bargaining

There are (3) government sectors in the collective bargaining world; Federal Sector, State and Local Sector, and Private Sector. I'll break them down here. I'm breaking them down to give the reader an understanding of each sector as it relates to negotiations.

Federal Sector: Consists of government agencies as employers with Federal sector Unions.
Here are some examples of Federal agencies: Social Security Administration (S.S.A.), Transportation Security Authority (T.S.A.), Department of Labor (D.O.L.), Veterans Administration (V.A.), Department of Treasury (D.O.T.) U.S. Postal Service (U.S.P.S.).

The Federal Sector is governed by the F.L.R.A. (page 117).

Here are a couple of examples of Federal Unions: American Federation of Government Employees (A.F.G.E.), National Treasury Employees Union (N.T.E.U.), which are two of the largest Federal sector unions. And (N.A.G.E.) National Association of Government Employees and (N.F.F.E.) National Federation of Federal Employees.

State and Local Sector: This consists of city and state or county agencies as the employers with State and Local sector Unions.
Here are some examples of State and Local agencies, State Roads Department, Transportation Authority, Fire Departments, Police

Departments, Public Works Department, Bureau of Prisons, Hospitals and Health Care Facilities.

Here are some examples of State and Local unions: American Federation of State County and Municipal employees (A.F.S.C.M.E.), International Association of Fire Fighters, (I.A.F.F.), Fraternal Order of Police (F.O.P.) City Union of Baltimore (C.U.B.), Amalgamated Transit Union (A.T.U.) and the Service Employees International Union (S.E.I.U.)"

The State and Local sector is governed by State and County laws and the N.L.R.A. (page 117).

Private Sector: Consists of private employers and the respective organized union locals.

Here are some examples of Private sector employers; "Northrup Grumman Corp., United Postal Service, (U.P.S.), Privately owned Hospitals, such as Johns Hopkins. Also, General Motors, Chrysler, Lockheed Martin, Boeing, Ford Corp, Airlines, Mining Companies, etc., Chemical Companies.

The private sector is governed by the N.L.R.A. (page 117).

Here are some examples of private-sector unions:

International Brotherhood of Teamsters (I.B.T.), United Steelworkers of America (U.S.W.A.), International Brotherhood of Electrical Workers (I.B.E.W.), Salaried Employees Association (S.E.A.) The United Auto Workers (U.A.W.), Airline Pilots (A.L.P.A.), United Mine Workers (U.M.W.), Sheet Metal Workers (S.M.W.), United Food and Commercial Workers (U.F.C.W.) and Boilermakers to name a few.

CHAPTER TEN
Federal Sector Bargaining

Now let's talk about the different aspects of Sector Bargaining and the associated leverages with each.

Federal Sector bargaining: This sector, as defined above, of government Agencies (management) and Unions, cannot bargain over wages or health care as the government preordains these. Still, there are laws on federal sector bargaining, as bargaining under a "condition of employment." The only leverage that labor or agencies have is by statute and Political action. Unlike the private sector, Federal sector bargaining is paid by the taxpayer via Congressional laws and acts. The bargaining leverage for both is cyclical and based on the current administration and legislative houses. Accordingly, any such change in a Federal law has a direct or even indirect impact on agencies and their respective Unions.

From the start of bargaining in the Federal Sector, the parties usually have several sessions called: Ground Rules, i.e., ground-rule negotiations, which consists of the location for negotiation, the schedule, number of negotiators, and subjects/articles of the Master Agreement that will be up for renegotiation. This ground rule bargaining could last several weeks or even longer. Then, after all of this and based on this, the parties start the Term Bargaining negotiations.

Federal sector unions cannot impose any action that affects commerce; no work stoppage, no sickouts, or another more familiar way, no strikes. They are illegal and not authorized in the government. Also, agencies cannot engage in a lockout.

If you're old enough, you may remember the Air Traffic Controller Strike of 1981? It was a Federal sector Union that defied a Federal Law. And the Union was decertified as a result. Even the National A F of L-C I O, took minimal action. As I understand it, the Professional Air Traffic Controller Organization (P.A.T.C.O.) held their selves higher than the Blue-Collar majority of the AFL-CIO. So, as a result, there was no full-court press by the AFL-CIO.

Federal sector bargaining consists of a condition of employment. Involving; employee rights, time & leave language, work schedules, grievance and arbitration articles, hours of work, merit promotion, employee awards and recognition, discipline, appraisals, official time, telework, equal employment opportunity, etc. Plus, a myriad of other contractual issues concerning the agency and employees. This term bargaining can go on for 3-6 months or longer, and some cases for years-depending on the complexity and number of issues/articles on the table.

During this time frame, as bargaining continues, with no agreement insight on one of the multiple issues, a Federal Mediator can be requested from the Federal Mediation and Conciliation Service (F.M.C.S.) (page 117), another Federal agency, set in place by Statute for federal sector bargaining. If mediation is not successful, the assigned mediator can release the parties to the Federal Service Impasse Panel (F.I.S.P.) (page 117), a Branch of the (Federal Labor Relations Authority (F.L.R.A.) page (117) for resolution. If issues (disagreements) are sent to F.S.I.P., the agency then makes a final and binding decision. And accordingly, all disputes are resolved and an order issued. Which then concludes the bargaining. It's the only avenue that the federal sector has to handle conflicts, as work stoppages/strikes in the federal sector are illegal. If during **Any** negotiations either party feels the other party is not bargaining in Good Faith, that party can go to the F.L.R.A. by filing an U.L.P.- page (118), Unfair Labor Practice action. The F.L.R.A. is the Federal Sector agency to handle such charges, wherein that agency reviews the complaint and makes the determining decision.

If the federal sector Unions and their respective agencies would get on the same page from a political standpoint, they could make very beneficial headway. Still, both parties battle upon each change in administrations as political appointees are put in place at the various agencies and have their political agenda.

I have witnessed evidence of the parties tirelessly working together, and when they do, the combined efforts always benefit the workers, the public, and the agency. Also, from the standpoint of a mediator, let me say that both parties work HARD for the employees they manage or represent. I have sat through many hours of hard-fought negotiations where the principal interest was the employees. I don't know if it's realized or appreciated by the employees or the general public to which they serve, but it is true.

An example of the need for government agencies, the employees, and their unions, can be stated as follows: *IF the government ever had a **total shutdown**,* the American public would suffer GREATLY! As in a complete government shutdown, the following essential agencies would be closed: Social Security Administration-meaning no S.S.A. checks processed and the Transportation Security Administration resulting in no security at airports, trains. No disrespect to the National parks, National Zoo, or any other similarly government-run agencies.

But as you can readily see, the Federal Sector is a critical sector of the prominent Three when you look at the agencies that are essential for both our economic and homeland security.

CHAPTER ELEVEN
State and Local Sector Bargaining

Now let's discuss the state and local sector, similar to the Federal Sector in that the Unions *in many states* cannot strike. State and Local bargaining, are governed by state laws, and they can be different depending on the State. The Fire Houses and Police Departments probably wouldn't strike if they could! Why? Because of YOU and Me, that's why. Their concern is for the safety of all of us, the workers in the counties and cities are paramount. That's why firefighters are the first to go into burning buildings. And why the police storm into the line of fire to save us! Accordingly, they are respected by the respective City Council and County Councils. Those more readily known in the state and local sector; Public Works, who manage the cities systems Safety divisions, monitor school children to and from school, and traffic safety across the city, plus City Hall, which controls all activity under the auspices of the Mayor. The transportation divisions in both cities and counties, to name only a few. These are the departments and employees that we count on every day of our lives.

Again, these groups, during contract bargaining, bargain hard. In these cases, negotiation is allowed for wages, although usually set by the respective county councils or city councils. The bargaining committees consist of the respective Labor Commissioners for the city and county and the respective Union leaderships. They have the latitude to bargain over upgrades and reclassification of employees, as another way to get monetary increases for the city and county employees. Again, after membership approval, the City Council or County Council must then approve the contract.

Some of the most known public sector employees are in transportation. Wherein the daily bus routes that take us back and forth to our jobs, busses that take us on excursions and tours across the country. These Mass Transit employers and their Unions take special pride in picking you up and delivering you safely to your destination. I know this because I have not only used such reliable transportation, but I have witnessed it personally as a Commissioner of Mediation and, more recently, as an Arbitrator.

Without the state and local sector employers and employees who serve the respective commuting workforces and overall day to night transportation needs, the cities and counties would come to a complete stop. So, when you are taking public transportation, greet the drivers with a smile and a thank you.

"There is an old saying; the easiest way to open any door is with a smile."

Daughters and Son, L-R, Melanie, Roy, Julie (just thought I'd use my children, they are a bright light and open many doors.)
The picture by union photographer St. Pete Beach, FL. 1996

CHAPTER TWELVE
Private Sector Bargaining

Now lastly, the private sector, a whole different circumstance in collective bargaining. If you ever heard the term, drastic action, work stoppage, or the phrase (a negative effect on Commerce,) it was most likely a direct result of a dispute between a private-sector labor Union and a Company.

Organized labor dates back to the 1800s. It grew, and the Nationwide desire to join a Union grew with it. It peaked around the 1960-70-time frame and started a downward trend in the 1990s.

Private sector bargaining is different in that they can halt commerce; A work stoppage (see page 34) to extract an agreement for issues that are in negotiations. Most collective bargaining negotiations end with no work stoppage and, most with a mutual understanding and agreement on how to move forward to better the employer and, accordingly, the employees.

The contract bargaining in the private sector is different in many regards then the Public and Federal sector bargaining. As in the Private sector, it's more of an independent process. The Union pays for its travel, per-diem, and the parties set the bargaining schedule/location by mutual agreement as a result. The atmosphere of the three sectors in negotiations, on the other hand, are very similar. Similar to stress, loud conversations, trust, preparation, and leverage review. Also identical in mutual respect at the end of the contract bargaining.

What happens at the start of a negotiation? Either the employer or union will send in a letter to open the Collective Bargaining Agreement (C.B.A.) page (112), starting the process, the communication than as to the bargaining schedule, location, and what sections/articles do the parties want to open for negotiations. The parties at the outset of the bargaining will exchange proposals—both in original hard copy form and then electronic with hard copies to follow.

Early on, several caucuses (page 111) will occur, looking over the proposals presented. Now strategy comes into play after applying C, knowledge of the issues, and particular need. Then preparation based on experience. Here is usually where each party learned what leverage they have or don't have. Sometimes the parties will remove/modify their proposals and use that for a bargaining chip (page 115). The relationship is critical here. *A good one and the negotiations can move through some sidebar discussion with each chief negotiator. Wherein some bases for proposals is explained via trust.*

A bad relationship things can deteriorate quickly, but even in a good one, sometimes an issue or issues on the recommendations can be either undoable for either party, this is when common sense should persevere. In reality, work stoppages are the last thing either an employer or union wants, but not always, see below.

1979 S.E.A. Union strike history files by Rodmen Nelson

A "Short Story" that took 52 days
We'll have them on their knees!

Around 40 years or so, the membership of a private-sector union voted to strike the Employer. The strike was over Upgrades! Yes, you heard right; the employer, due to competition in its business, had to increase the wages of individual employees by raising the entry-level (hiring level), which then impacted other classifications by also elevating them.

This particular Union leadership felt that more classifications, effecting more employees, should be included in this wage-classification upgrade. The employer felt that what they were doing was necessary to grow its business, and to do any more would be a detriment. As the discussions continued, the farther apart they became. Eventually, as required by the Union's By-Laws, there was a meeting of the membership calling to vote either to strike the employer or not. At that time, the By-Laws required a simple majority to authorize a strike. For example, if the bargaining unit was 100 members, 51 could authorize a strike. In this reference, if the vote reached a simple majority of 50 plus one, it would authorize a strike. The actual vote in this story was around 482 yea 435 nays. From that particular leadership, out came the infamous statement; "We'll drive them to their knees!"

This is where you become familiar with; boiled polish sausage hot dogs, and Entenmann's donuts! As this is a regular meal on the picket line. For this local, this was the second strike in 4 years the last 1975 (page 66). Which was a (1) one-week strike over Mandatory Overtime, of which there was no mandatory contract language in that particular C.B.A. That strike resolved with the terminated employee returned to work and a "Strike Settlement," agreement written up. Now coming off that success, I imagine the ego enlarged, and therefore, this strike in 1979.

This story is told in hindsight as there was **no leverage** here for the Union. I mean you're striking over, "upgrades," not a termination as in 1975, discussed herein in a later chapter. In that work stoppage, the entire membership became as one, as no one wanted to be terminated for refusing to work O/T when the contract had no such requirement. Here there **was the leverage!**

This strike, however, had no such leverage, and after over 50 plus days, the Union due to pressure from its members voted to return to work.

What memorialized this effort was a;
Monogrammed Pin with the # 52 on it! ☺

Here is an even funnier ending to commemorate the strike; the strike was well over, and the then Union President was talking at a dinner for a retiring member of management. The discussion of the work stoppage and the Pin above came up. The argument between the manager and Union President was whether the time on strike was 51 days or 52? After a lengthy discussion and no agreement, the Union said they would file a grievance! ☺☺

A Top song in 1979, "Sad Eyes," that was certainly apropos.

CHAPTER THIRTEEN
Negotiation Results

On the next page, in 1986 at our convention, *as National Vice President of the F.I.S.U., discussing recent contract negotiations,* at that time, with over 45 affiliates (page 112) across the *country in some nine states. We termed it the "Umbrella" Negotiations, as it covered all of our member affiliates.* **That year a top hit was; "Say You, Say Me,"** as we shared with our respective memberships the contracts we negotiated. Our National Union represented the entire spectrum of classifications, such as mail clerks, stenographers, production coordinators, design drafters, machinists, carpenters, plumbers, illustrators, photographers, tool designers, engineering aides, five different classifications of technicians, planners, associate engineers, and Fellow Engineers.

These negotiations involved multi-million-dollar contracts. Bargaining with at the time one of the world's largest electronic and nuclear companies, which took place over a 4-6-week time frame. Our committee housed in a hotel reviewing and making proposals and counter-proposals. We were continually making telephonic messages after each session, updating the workforce. In the private sector, as we were, all our expenses were paid by the Union, including hotel, per diem, travel, copying, etc.

After reaching a "handshake" agreement and preparing a brief synopsis of the contract negotiations, our committee departed returning to their respective states and setting up their local membership meetings for approving or disapproving the negotiated contract. Upon acceptance of the negotiated agreement, the parties agreed to print copies of the C.B.A. for distribution to managers and union members.

In addition to this National Contract bargaining, My Union also represented another employer, Thompson C.G.R., (Company of General Radiology), a French medical imaging company. Sometimes both the national contract bargaining and this local bargaining was happening simultaneously. These were different contract negotiations regarding wages, pension, health care, and work processes.

The photo during the 1986 National Union convention.

SHORT STORY
Nothing Leaves This Room!

As a Union or Management leader, there may be a time or times that during some negotiation that you may have to take a caucus ("separate discussion" page 111) with your negotiating team. There may also be a time when the "caucus" takes place in the next room, which could take place in the company/agency's Human Resources department. Or, in the Union hall, where the negotiations are taking place.

During one such negotiation, around 1996, I had assembled my bargaining team in the next room in the employer's facility for a caucus. At which time, I used the room grease board to write some key issues. Making note as to the priority of each subject and remarking on the need for its leverage. There were several issues that I put up on the board. We had ensuing questions/comments, and each bargaining member's task to present to management upon resuming the meeting with them.

Specific issues were for the negotiating committee's eyes only. These were critical, and I made each member understand the importance, so emphasized that **NOTHING Leaves this ROOM!** Everyone agreed. So, at that point, I started to remove the issues from the employer's grease board. Then disaster struck! No, the room wasn't tape-recorded. No, there was not a window for anyone to view the writing on the board. No, it was worst, I had used a **PERMANENT MARKING PEN!!**

So, now in a panic mode, I could not get the writing off the damn board. ☹ Committee members used soda, water, and finally, one member tipped a napkin in their coffee, and the coffee removed the confidential writing☺ Whew, it was true that nothing would leave that room. The negotiations resumed, with signs of additional stress on our faces. But upon leaving that day, was a chorus of smiles all around.

A top song that year; Nobody Knows. *And nobody did, thank God!*

CHAPTER FOURTEEN
Running a Meeting

Remember, when I mentioned, early in the book (page xvi) about trying to emulate someone when developing your negotiating skills? Well, in this chapter, I am going to share some techniques that I learned through observation. Before I get into those, let's discuss you and a case where you are running a meeting as a first chair or lead negotiator.

First of all, be on time. If you know what the meeting is about to make preparations, for your position. If you don't know, think about the worst-case scenario! Ok, and this primarily refers to the Union committee.

The management committee is usually more disciplined in this type of setting. More disciplined in that only one person talks at a time with no interruptions. The management committee usually has a note-taker.

Follow that process, have someone ready to take notes; that person should be there only for that purpose. With this method, someone is not part of the discussion and then loses critical comments in the note-taking process. Talk to your committee in advance to let them know, no breaking in the middle of a conversation, let the person, manager, or union finish their comment and, more importantly, answer the question posed.

Take a caucus if necessary, make those brief and few. As you should all already be, what was that I said? Oh yeah, be prepared! That's it. Set a mental or written list of items to be discussed. If you don't know an answer, then respond, as maybe you heard before, "I'll get back to you." Sound familiar?

41

As a chair, **you** control your committee and the meeting, keep focused on the issue at hand, and do not let anyone move you off your topic by going into another direction. It is a tactic that is sometimes used in bargaining of any issue, remember that. Stay on track.

At the end of each session or the session, have a sign-off procedure. Get an agreement before the meeting about the note-taker(s) and, at the very least, set a time frame (24 hours/next morning, etc.) to review the typed-up minutes so they can be signed and set aside. Do this at each session; it develops a history of the negotiations. And it is invaluable; they're called "bargaining notes."

Now here are some (Union) meeting tactics I learned through observation:

First one: Now, you are running a meeting, and someone raises their hand to be recognized—the intent to disrupt the meeting or set it in a different direction.

So, here is how you handle this: Let the person say their thought, listen, and when they finish, do not respond; just thank them and immediately recognize another person! Just let that person sit back down, and you are, in a way ignoring their thought by directly going to another person. It works.

Second one: Now, let's say the same person or someone else; it does not matter. That person raises their hand to be recognized. And when identified, they make a motion on some action or study—moving it to a committee. It is another attempt to set the meeting off into another direction or just simply to make a motion on an issue of little relevance.

So, here is how you handle this: As chair, you appoint **that** person as a Committee of ONE To investigate and report back at a future meeting. It puts the issue right back where it belongs; to the person who made the motion.

Third one: The contract was just negotiated, and the meeting set for a vote. <u>In this scenario,</u> there was no mail-out ballot, but a secret ballot at the meeting. On the agenda was one other thing; a due's increase! Now, as the Chair, you should have the "grapevine" information as to how each issue will be accepted. You hear that there will be opposition to the dues increase and that one person, in particular, will stand to shoot it down.

<u>So, here is how you handle this:</u> You never argue from the head table. You reach out before the meeting and elect someone with the backbone to be ready for the dues challenge. When the person rises to contest the due's increase, the person you asked to counter the argument raises their hand. You now recognize that person who then argues on behalf of the due's increase, against the person trying to shoot it down. Did you ever see someone stick a pin in a balloon at a party...? Well, that is pretty much the result.

Lesson: Preparation...or how about "Advanced Preparation, based on information!"

Keep in mind that these situations are for those who may want to disrupt or set a meeting in a different direction. Not for those sincere people.

CHAPTER FIFTEEN
Sharing Experience-Knowledge

Here is a question, is it a smart or helpful action to help the person sitting on the opposite side of the table? Should you? Well, let's put this into perspective with another history lesson:

Here is a story that now dates back over 40 years, involving two high-level leaders in the Labor-Management world of negotiations. One was relatively young and inexperienced, and the other one was well up in both age and experience. As these two competitors (by positions held) sparred with each other during contract negotiations, during one contract negotiation, an item arose that the experienced leader recognized as a weakness in his opponent knowledge.

What to do? It would be easy to bury or embarrass the less experienced negotiator, and not only that but would have strengthened the bargaining position of the elder. So, there they are in a meeting with each chairing their respective committees. What to do? Do you take advantage of the less experienced negotiator, or do you seize the opportunity to help the opposing chair out of the predicament? Why? That person may not even be there in the next series of contract bargaining anyway, what the hell? Hey, it is not the more experienced negotiator's job to help the adversary. Let that person learn by mistakes like everyone else had to! Right?

What? What would you do, *before turning the page* think about it? Think about what approach you would take.

Hey, this is not a personality, psychology, or ego test, but just a true story on what happened.

It went the way of the more experienced bargainer helping, the less experienced one out of an embarrassing moment. It was done confidentially in a one on one sidebar.

So, what is the definition of one on one? (page 109) You got it. This story thereby developed a 20-plus year mutual respect and admiration between the two bargaining adversaries with the reaching out to help not bury. I'm sure you can reason what the benefit was for the elder. First, it was the self-satisfaction of not exploiting another. If nothing else, that was enough, but there were times that this good deed helped solidify the next couple plus decades of bargaining both locally and nationally.

Ok, what did you decide?

CHAPTER SIXTEEN
Used Car Negotiations

Negotiating, it is in every walk of your life. Now, what are some essential ingredients to negotiation? Well, there are several; one is research before you try to WIN a deal in negotiating, do your research. If you are buying a used car, check the competitor's pricing, matching, age mileage, model, looks both exterior and interior. What is the mileage on the tires, not just on the vehicle, what is the repair history, was it a rental, etc. Hey, you are going to have this vehicle for several years, so take your time!

Once you have that information, then go into action. You want to negotiate down to what works for YOU, not to what the used car dealer wants. Remember the name; used car **"Dealer"** didn't come from osmosis. Also, remember that the world of technology is at your fingertips. There is no excuse for not being prepared to negotiate. Time IS $$ in manufacturing, in retail, and negotiations.

As I go on, I need to mention the following; Be prepared for the worst-case scenario. So, let me expand on that. What would be a worst-case situation?

First, you missed the (Window of Opportunity), and someone else got the car. **Second,** you either did not verify that you had the funds to close a deal, or you didn't make sure you could get the required car insurance. **Third,** and it doesn't get much worst that this; you didn't do the research and, once buying the car, neglected to have it inspected by a trustworthy mechanic, thereby missing the usual 30-day window for used car warranties only to discover a significant engine problem! Now I know you will agree, this would be the Worst-Case Scenario, exclaiming; Jumping Jehosafat's!

Once at a car lot, remember the process; you're in the driver's seat **before** you get into the driver's seat. Check out the selected car (carfax) cross-reference other dealers with similar vehicles, for price comparisons. Start the bargaining, **be ready to, hmm....?. walk, that's it.** Negotiate your price then mention that you have a trade-in. Before you bring it in, have it cleaned and the engine detailed. That cost you'll add to the deal. Also, try and bargain for the warranty. You can ask for free oil changes for a specified period, how about car washes, don't limit yourself. If you have to, let them see your ass walking. Wait for the "hey, come back here." Then let me know how you did!

Picture in September 2019 of a used car lot.

CHAPTER SEVENTEEN
Used Car, My Bargaining Example.

Ok, you the know the saying, "why don't you practice what you preach?" well, this is why I am adding this chapter to the book. About three years ago, when driving my car, a Congressional Series Lincoln Town Car, another motorist came through the red signal and hit my front right bumper as I was turning on a green. No one was hurt, so that was good news! My car now not drivable, and later to find out the damage to the front end was not repairable, so my insurance allowed me a rental car.

I started looking online for another Lincoln, I came across two such vehicles both 2011 (The last year for the Town car) and both had about 30,000 in mileage, both Black on Black, but two very different prices. One was at $26,499, and the other one at $23,499 a $3000 price difference. The lower price one was about 30 miles away and the higher price within a couple of miles. I looked at both vehicles inside and out very comparable. No difference that I could view. Asked for the car facts on both (has it been in an accident, water damage, was it a rental, etc.) still no remarkable difference.

Now the negotiations began; I told the Used Car manager and sales representative at the dealership of the higher-priced car, that this other dealer, had the same car for about $3000 less! There were usually back and forth arguments, but I was going to purchase a Lincoln from whoever would meet my price. Suffice it to say my last words concerning the higher-priced vehicle were; *"I am renting a car, and the rental lease will expire in 7 more days. I am going to be in another Lincoln by then. So, let me make it clear, make up your mind. I am buying your car at 3000 dollars less, or am I going to the other dealer? Either way, I am going to be in a Lincoln Town car before the rental expires!"*

I purchased the Lincoln Town car priced at $26499 for $23499, plus I was able to negotiate a "bumper to bumper warranty" for a reasonable price. Here is the bottom line; Know when to keep talking, know when to start walking. I did it, and you can do it too. Now let's look at the following chapter on your negotiating skills.

Lesson: Knowledge

The picture was taken of my new Lincoln by the negotiator, me!

Oh, by the way, a **Top song in 2016, "Love Yourself,"** which I did after this purchase.

CHAPTER EIGHTEEN
Now You're the Negotiator

So, you just got some $$ from the I.R.S. income refund. Twenty percent of the people will put it into savings, but the rest of us (Smiling) will go to purchase a household item. It may be new bedding, sofa, dining room set, hey and let's not forget that Car! Can you use what you've learned so far to get the best deal possible?

Let's see if it is a used car, then go back a couple of paragraphs and review. A new car has a warranty and price reduction usually built-in. Right? Does that stop you from researching with another dealer? No, it doesn't and should not, what will you be losing some time, phone calls, etc.! You choose. Remember the title 'Know when to keep talking; know when to start walking."

Sometimes you can get some benefit from your trade-in before you take the car into the dealer to look it over. Do some things, spend some money to have your vehicle detailed, **especially the engine**. (Hey that's what "Used Car Dealers) do!

Usually around $225.00, but you should get that back in trade in money. Just add it to what you're asking. You are in the driver seat, first figuratively and then literally.

Now you are in the new or preowned car that you just negotiated, and you are feeling pretty good about yourself and driving to the furniture store. Remember, always go in with the attitude that you don't need anything. Your sofa is ok, etc. Remember they need to sell you! Hey, don't get your price; "start walking" there is more than one furniture store. It is up to you. Take your time, think about the picture in the store that was placed there just over the sofa you want. Do you go ahead and say what the hell and buy it, or do you use the sale of the couch to get a better deal on the picture, maybe? Or did you ask if they are going to throw in a couple of lamps? Make them an offer they can't refuse; I am ready to purchase, are you prepared to sell?

Don't bargain and you'll go home *with what they want to sell you*!

Here is a note: Remember when I said sometime in life, you would be up against a negotiator "better than you." Well, the point here is, DON'T LET the sales manager see the **need** in your face. They look to read expressions. So, practice with your spouse or friend before you start the bargaining. I'm telling you this will work, and you will get what you want and save $$. Hey, do you think the sales clerk is giving away their desire to sell? The old saying "practice makes perfect" didn't just float down from a cloud!

Ok, here is another ACE in your pocket. If you can buy with cash, remember the tax refund. Let whomever the sales clerk is know that you have Cash! Use it to your advantage and use it as leverage, remember that word?

Hey, how about that new bed? Now, remember you, "DON'T NEED IT." Negotiate as such, and when you get the price down to your need, you'll thank yourself when they deliver it. Hey, you negotiated FREE delivery, right? Realizing the $$$ you saved. Don't forget to read the warranty, especially on the multi-position, motorized beds. Oh, get that in writing and **read it.** Know the difference between a "Limited and Unlimited Warranty? No, you won't know until you ask, what are the "limitations?"

After doing that, you'll get the best night's sleep of your life!

CHAPTER NINETEEN
Another Negotiating Technique

Here is yet another technique in negotiations. I have been explaining how, when buying an item that you should not show the sales associate your need! Remember? Well, here is another tactic, its a method using reverse negotiating skills.

For this example: Let's say your house needs new windows, some can't open, some can't stay open, or yours are not double-paned, and they let cold air in the winter and cold air out in the summer. Maybe you just want to update your home with brand new windows period.

In most states, there are very reputable window contractors. There are periods of the year that are most favorable for installation, which is usually followed by discounts offered. Right?

Now let's go back to my used car negotiations. Remember, when I told the dealer

"I'm going to be in a Lincoln Town car before my rental car expires.", well in this negotiation for new windows, you can use that same tactic. To perspective contractors: "I am going to have new windows installed by __?__give a date. So, you (contractor) decide; the one that gives me the best price/warranty will be at my home installing windows! A direct and dominant position. Feels good, doesn't it?

So, you see, this is different than buying a sofa as you will need free estimates, and each contractor will then know the need and conditions of your windows. But, in that case, it does not matter because you will be using a more robust approach, and believe me, it will work. You still have to know when to "start walking." Or you sit in your house and let them start walking.

Understanding the different types of negotiations is essential, and both are laid out here for you. **You are always** in the driver's seat; remember that and use these skills, and you will save yourself $$.

*Oh, by the way, DON'T forget to ask which contractor offers Military/ Veterans discounts, **after you get the final quote!***

CHAPTER TWENTY
May I speak to the Manager!

I wanted to add another negotiating technique. When you reach an impasse with the sales representative, and it happens. Ask to speak with the manager. This might be met with some resistance, as no first-level sales clerk or section supervisor wants to have their manager step in. But you're not there to satisfy the salesperson but to satisfy your wants. When the manager arrives on the scene, marry your request with politeness. Have you ever climbed a ladder? Well, think of a circumstance as climbing a ladder; each rung is a higher-level manager. If still no resolution, you can ask for yet a higher-level manager.

Now you must have the resolution in mind. Be ready to present it, whether it's a lower price or warranty or an item that was supposed to be delivered but is still en route! If it's a price, have your comparable information as an argument. And cite it, see Chapter 17 my used car example. As I've mentioned early on, be prepared, what's the worst-case scenario with the situation at hand." If it's a delivery and the item is damaged, access the cost or appearance and your need. Bargain a reduced price based on the specific damage. If you can wait for a better piece, have it returned and call the? You guessed it, the manager! Due to the inconvenience, you can ask for something to address this inconvenience. Weigh it, and use a reasonable, common-sense approach.

Always remember to use the leverage you have, preparation will give you that answer. Be ready to walk, if you follow this you be home with a smile on your face and a happier pocketbook!

CHAPTER TWENTY-ONE
Back to Contract Bargaining

In Term Bargaining; (the duration of the contract). You also have what is called "mid-term" bargaining (bargaining in between the start and termination of contract). So, you are either in contract negotiations for a new or revised agreement or in mid-term, where issues may arise either initiated by the employer/agency or the union. Something that one party wants as an improvement and does not want to wait until the next term, which could be years away. If it is a one-party desire that usually will result in some give and take or Quid Pro Quo. If it is a mutual desire, want, or need, then the bargaining; give and take probably already considered or included.

So, each party must give weight to its *need* versus the *give*. Remember the A.B.C.s, and let's start in reverse with C. preparation, knowledge, worst-case scenario. Make sure to apply all of these before A. & B. kick in! Go back and remind yourself and your colleagues about the importance of A & B.

Preparation, preparation, preparation, this is how you learn your leverage and your opponent's leverage. From here, you develop bargaining strategies. Don't forget, based on your advantage, to prioritize your issues/needs/wants.

Bargaining Committee

Hand out assignments to each of your committee members, give these assignments based on the strength of your respective committee members. For example, if a member is unusually good on the computer, let that person check out seniority, age, and other profiles of the bargaining unit. If a member is skilled at writing, let that person create the contract language proposals. If a person is competent in communication, let that member deliver the negotiation status, etc. You have to do your internal assessment also.

For the management/employer, what are you hearing from your first-level and middle-level managers? As they must work with the C.B.A. each day throughout the contract. Record their wants versus their needs versus what's doable in the upcoming negotiations. Remember, they are the first line of offense and defense; they are the ones that lead on the employer's behalf. You must give them the tools they need to administer the C.B.A. accurately. While also supervising the employees.

As for the Union leadership, the goal is similar, in fact, probably more alike than you realize. Both parties want to strengthen the C.B.A. on their behalf. Sometimes after the exchange of the initial proposals, you may find that there is room for transfer of wants, making the negotiation move more smoothly, and this is where the experience and expertise in bargaining come forward and also the relationship. Of course, that is not always the case. More likely is the same contract language that the parties want to strengthen on their behalf, which is something that they both want, which then causes the struggle, and usually, the party with the "leverage" wins!.

There are usually many months before bargaining starts, and each party is aware of the needs of the other, and here is where the respective strategies make either a successful or unsuccessful negotiation. So, how do you prepare when you know there will be similar needs, especially when that struggle will result in more forceful language for one and weaker for the other?

Well, here are some thoughts: You might have to trade off other sections of the contract for a particular need. You may have to dream up something that is not currently part of C.B.A. but could be added. Or something that was part of a prior conversation either during a grievance meeting or local midterm meeting. You can call this thinking, "Out of Box." Let me throw out a "for instance" example.

Example

Let's just say the conflict in need is: The number of issues that can be grieved. In other words, **"covered** items." (page116) The employer proposes to reduce the number of covered topics, and the Union aims to increase the number of covered issues. Let's take this a step further; the Union did not prepare for this as it was unexpected! Remember, "worst-case scenario," Well, you cannot always be ready. Sometimes you have to address the issue as it is presented; this is when each party must look at other parts of the C.B.A. to see if something unaddressed on other negotiations can be used to work this *tough situation* out.

What to do? Remember, this is just a (for instance) situation, and this is just a (for example) remedy. We have to look at who has the leverage in this situation. The one with the advantage need not work as hard as the other.

The party in the weaker position must now look at some other less critical issues to give up. In this situation, you are looking at a loss somewhere in the contract, so what can you lose that is not as painful? Maybe you rationalize that giving up some covered items is not that bad. If so, take advantage of that and try to get some other language like How about 1. If the covered topics are reduced, suggesting the employer pick up additional meetings or preparation costs for the Union? 2. Adding a step to the grievance procedure that includes Last Chance language? 3. Something farther removed from this Section? 4. A percentage of the company's stock issued to employees as a bonus? 5. An incentive program for perfect attendance? 6. How about clearing employees' absences at the beginning of each year? Or if it's not already in your proposals. How about an **article on the "Job**

Security" language in case of a plant closure? A wording that gives a reduced age and service retirement for pensions due to a sale of a plant closure. I trust you get the idea and need for preparation and or innovative thinking, depending on the circumstance.

Lesson: Preparation.

Here is a rule: Treat each bargaining like there will be many more. Leave each bargaining session with respect, respect of your adversary, with their admiration of you, and, most importantly, respect in yourself.

RESPECT

GIVE IT

to

Get it!

CHAPTER TWENTY-TWO
Worst Case Scenario

Remember this, ALWAYS prepare for a worst-case scenario no matter what you are bargaining over. Think to yourself. What is the worst that could happen, what is the worst outcome? If you do this as I did it for the last five decades, then you will be prepared. A history lesson: As I stated, I always prepared and asked myself that question, "what's the worst that could happen." One time and one time only did I get blindsided.

It's was around 1988, and now the Union President of the referenced local, I had approximately just under 3,000 bargaining unit members between Westinghouse and Thomson (C.G.R.), a medical imaging employer. I was always attempting to negotiate upgrades for the various departments that I represented. This one singular occasion, I had an ongoing negotiation when the Department Head Manager and I had agreed upon reclassification of some 50 plus employees. All at differing levels of upgrades.

So, what was so great about this? The requirement for upgrades was based on newly demonstrated skill levels required in the job duties. Plus, even more importantly, the Wage and Salary department, a separate division of the company was also ready to sign off on the increase. As without there concurrence, it was a no go.

So, here I go to sign the upgrades and reclassifications with the Department Head and Human Resources Management. A done deal, right? As I get to the meeting the Department Head had a sick look on his face, the H.R. manager also seemed perplexed and had his head hanging down. That is when the Department Head handed me a letter from the corporate office.

It read in part, "The department is being closed!" All of the employees previously believing to receive promotions with $$$ were now going to terminated!!! Wow!

Wow is right. A vast understatement if there ever was one.

But I don't want to leave it here, as I'm writing this book and this does have a happy ending.

The decision from corporate after much lobbying by the Department Head and with whatever pressure I could apply, the decision was changed. Now due to that collective effort, not as many upgrades happened. There were some employees upgraded at the lower levels a few at the top. And, no one lost their job!

After that situation, I added it to my worst-case scenarios, possibilities.

Hey, the **1988 top song was, "Never Going to Give Up,"** *How's that?*

Lesson: Be prepared.

SHORT STORY
Leverage

I've mentioned throughout this writing about the A, B, C's of negotiations. In C, there is preparation, knowledge, worst case, common sense, and leverage. In this story, I'm describing a situation about contract negotiations, an impasse, and following **a 1975 strike.**

The issue over an employee terminated for refusing to work overtime.

In this particular C.B.A., there was no language on mandatory overtime. Employees could work as much overtime that was available and approved or not work any overtime, with no need for a reason. This contract had been in effect since the late 1930s, and parties had a relatively harmonious labor-management relationship. That is until this issue.

So, let us look at the A, B, C's. Due to the previous good working relationship, the; A, and B, _Trust, Word, and Integrity were of no issue._ And it wasn't in this case either.

Preparation: as far as preparation, the union did its due diligence; it called for a membership meeting to authorize drastic action (strike). The issue was explained, and the Union leadership asked for support to authorize a strike against the employer. The membership was keenly aware of the problem due to earlier communication(s) by the union. The members were worried that they too could be terminated for not working overtime and, as a result, gave the Union leadership an overwhelming vote for a strike.

Knowledge; The union base on those earlier communications and the feedback that they were getting knew that calling for a strike authorization meeting would have the positive results they needed.

Worst case scenario; what's the worst-case scenario, 1st a negative vote not authorizing the strike, which they were not concerned. 2nd if the leadership took no action on this highly contentious issue, none of the administration would survive reelection!

Common Sense rational; This would come to bear during the ensuing work stoppage and the strike settlement agreement if one. Common sense is to bargain what's needed to resolve the strike and not end up with an "empty bag."

Leverage; In this case, the union due to the total support of its membership-had all the leverage they needed. The employer recognized the support and, as smart employers often do, decided to move this issue to the next round of term bargaining.

Results; After one long week on strike, the parties reached a strike settlement agreement wherein the terminated employee was returned to work. And the parties also reviewed several open grievances. Resolved many and re-solidified their relationship.

Oh, the **Top song that year, "Love Will Keep Us Together,"** and it did in this case!

Lesson: Preparation, Knowledge=Leverage

Note; During the current labor relations in the U.S.A., with few exceptions, the parties settle many disputes either by arbitration, mediation, or ongoing labor-management committees and good common sense, in determining their leverage.

SHORT STORY
The Quid Pro without the Quo

One day I get a call from a top-level manager asking to meet on an issue that was of interest to him. Now, as local Union President, I always was looking for a way to get upgrades for the members that I represented. Accordingly, we met, and after the usual "how are things" conversation, we got into the crux of the meeting.

The employer has two separate progressions or ladders (page 113) of similar tasks/job responsibilities. One progression/ladder had about 80 employees in the engineering world working in primarily one of the employer's eleven facilities. The similar progression/ladder had approximately 250 employees production/manufacturing world that worked in basically all of the facilities of the employer. As stated, the employer had eleven sites/facilities. The primary site encompassed three extensive facilities that were interconnected. Employees could walk from building to building by enclosed connections.

The other eight-plus facilities were spread out and needed transportation to visit. As President, I had members in every site. This manager began by saying, "as you are aware, there are two separate progressions/ladders of employees doing similar work, one group in the engineering department and the other group in the production department." I nodded. He continued, "I would like to be able to move the 80 employees throughout the 11 sites as needed just as the production department employees do." And I understand that there are issues concerning (work cross over) and the seniority issues from one group to the other that we will have to iron out."

I responded, 'yes, there are. Specifically, the different pay levels, the engineering group have a lower level of compensation that would have to be corrected. I continued, so we'd have to look at the 80 employees that are at various levels of pay to bring them in line with the employees in production." As the discussion continued, we agreed to go back, talk it over with our constituents and reconvene at a later date. My constituents would be my Executive Board and the area union representatives from both ladders/progressions."

One Month Later

Back at the bargaining table with the results of our constituents. We both had good news, my review was received well, and the manager was ready to "put to paper" our potential agreement; As follows: *The employer can move the progression of engineering to all eleven cites. The Union would receive upgrades for that progression equal to the production/manufacturing progression.*

A Case closed, right? Well, yes, it was for the Union.

Four Months Later!

I received another call from the manager, "need to meet today!" Ok, so we set up the meeting for later that day at lunch. When I arrived, the manager was steaming! "What?" I responded. He said, "I think I got screwed!" "How in the hell did you get screwed?" I asked. "You got the opportunity to move the engineering progression all over the 11 sites. That's what you wanted, right?"

He replied, "YES, but no one has moved/transferred to any of the other sites." So, I said, "That's not my problem." "True, but none of the supervisors have moved any of the 80 employees to other sites!", he said. With a smile on my face, I said: "Yes, I knew that they wouldn't (as no supervisor wants/lose or let his/her employees away from their direct supervision); that is why I agreed. But, I followed you are THE BOSS, so order them to move the employees."

A return smile and we finished our lunch. Many years later, the upgraded employees started slowly to transition to other sites, but never to the extent agreed to. So, I guess you could say this ended up being a one-sided agreement, but there is an old saying; Keep the relationship amicable and live to bargain another day! Which we did, but this was the Quid and Pro without the Quo.

Lesson: Knowledge

Oh, by the way, the **Year was 1994 a Top Song was; Hero!** Which is what I felt like after this negotiation, and so did the 80 upgraded employees.

CHAPTER TWENTY-THREE

You Have to A.S.K.!
Especially Veterans/Military discounts

Another $$$ savings without negotiating. Discounts. <u>However, you have to mention it!</u> That's doubly sure for V.A./Military discounts. **You have to ask!** Remember, the title of this book, "Know when to keep talking." So, when you are at the cash register, remember to ask, "do you give Veteran/Military discounts?" Hey, better that money in your pocket you/they earned.

Sometimes you will get we only recognize the Veterans for discounts on the Veteran's Day holiday at which sometimes, I sarcastically reply, oh yes, that's the only time the military fought was on Veteran's Day. Still, the person at the register cannot help that; it is the company. So, I haven't listed here in the eateries and stores that offer a Veteran's discount **year-round.** But either by going online or asking while at that particular restaurant or department store, you can quickly find out.

I didn't want it to turn into another, "no good deed goes unpunished," by listing some by not all, etc.!

So, in addition to whatever your buying/negotiating, remember, always ask about any discounts, and if you are a Veteran, don't forget to ask, "do you give Veteran/military discounts?"

In mediation 2005

Just for laughs!

As a labor advocate and commissioner of mediation, I have entered a tense situation from either labor or management more than once. When someone would speak up and said," It's not that we can't do it; it's the <u>Principal</u> damn it." At which time, I would respond, "What's the **Vice** <u>Principal</u> say?"

What to avoid!

I had mentioned that when I taught classes on contract interpretation, advanced contract interpretation, steward-supervisor, and relationship training, that I tried to share with the attendees, some experiences that they should avoid. So, here in Chapter 24 are a few.

Then I after that, I have added a couple of real-life and fun, "Short Stories." I hope you enjoy them as much as I had living and writing them

CHAPTER TWENTY-FOUR
What to avoid

1. Remember there is always TOMORROW, keep the relationship amicable.
2. **Why?** Because, unless you're retiring on Friday or have just received notice that you won the Power Ball. In labor-management relations, you'll most likely, have to go back and ask for something of the same person you just shouted out the day before!

   Oh, and by the way, make sure you have the winning Power Ball #s before you go jumping up and down on the boss's desk...only to find out you are missing a number!!! Hey, does that sound like a "Worst case scenario?" There is only one day during the year that you could do that and maybe get away with it! April 1st!
3. Which brings up, preparation for the worst case. How? Think of all the bad possibilities!
4. Be <u>clear on your request.</u> Getting what you asked for doesn't help if it isn't what you meant to ask.
5. **Don't miss** any contractual **time limits**! You can do that by having "Knowledge" of the contract, remember the **C** in negotiation, "preparation, <u>knowledge,</u> worst case, and common sense?" Your most substantial issue could be lost due to missing a time limit.
6. Avoid making empty threats. Or you could come up with an "empty bag."
7. Don't bluff. Support what you're discussing with facts, not a *loud voice.

   *The less sound one's argument, the louder the discussion.

8. Admit when you're wrong. What? I can't believe I said that. As I've never been wrong, **I'm smiling**. But, admitting a mistake will add to your character. Must be true as I've been called a character! (Making fun of yourself also is a character trait, a good one.)

9. Prepare each case or position, as if you'll go before a higher level. Rehearse/review anything you put in writing. Always keep it professional and accurate.

10. Enter a situation with a smile, not an attitude, try it, and you'll come out with a smile.

SHORT STORY
Contract Mediation
Shut up-you shut up-you shut the ----up!

So, what we have here is a 'Failure to Communicate." A large Federal Sector Agency and a massive Federal Sector Union face off in contract negotiations, facilitated by myself, then a Commissioner of Mediation. It's late in the evening, and the parties had been together in "term bargaining" for over a month. As the stress of negotiations took its toll, the tempers began to rise. An issue on the table was being discussed, at which point, the opposing side, said, "shut up." Followed by you, "shut up." Followed by no you, "shut the ----up! And continuing, get the picture? Anyway, after this quite a lengthy dialogue...no it wasn't dialogue but a vocal competition, as a mediator I called an end to this session to resume the next morning.

The next morning. As the bargainers took their respective seats, the atmosphere in the room, frigid, I opened with, "All of you got me in trouble last evening. As you'll remember, it ended with a series of "shut up, you shut up, no you shut the f----up!" So, leaving that meeting, my mind still remembering. As I got home, my wife said, good evening honey, what do you want for dinner? I said, "Shut the-----up!" So, I'm on PBJ all week.

Lesson; if you can somehow break the ice, add a little levity to the situation; it helps remind everyone that there is life after contract bargaining. Remember, keep the relationship amicable for the next set of negotiations.

P.s. Oh, by the way, you know, I never said that when I got home.

SHORT STORY
Strike on Monday! Back on Tuesday!

This yet another true story. From the memory files of this mediator. There was a local company employing around 35 employees. The negotiators, after several days of bargaining with an impasse on the horizon, requested the assistance of mediation. The issues on the table only a few; The wages and the introduction of a 401k savings plan. The Union committee of about eight employees wanted an increase in pay only. As this committee was relatively young, the issue of a 401k saving plan was not a priority to them.

So fast forward to a Friday afternoon and despite the best efforts of the mediator, the employer, and Union lead negotiator. The membership voted to strike effective that Monday morning! Which happened to be in the late fall of the year, and all of the Union committee members were hunters. So, the first thought was, this strike could go through the Deer season sometime in January.

The members were, "Ready," they had a cooler filled with beer and sodas a grill, and a 50 gal drum for a fire to keep warm on the picket line. It sounds like everything was a go for a long strike, right? Then the mediator asked a question of this 100% male membership.

Question? "How many of you are married?" Almost all the hands went up. I smiled and turned to the Union chief and said, "this strike will not last long!" Why was the response? Because I said, "we have the Thanksgiving Holiday and Christmas coming up, and when the wives start asking how are we going to pay for Christmas.... etc."

The strike lasted the entire 24-hour day of Monday, with almost a unanimous vote to return to work on Tuesday!

In this case, there was, "Leverage," but it was at home.

CHAPTER TWENTY-FIVE
An empty Bag!

Another story about contract bargaining. During contract negotiations, which was going into its 3rd week. An issue arose concerning the companies' attendance policy where the bargaining discussions saw back and forth proposals. One Union proposal would add compensation for those employes with excellent attendance. Combined with language to eliminate any "short illness," loopholes that employees could now get around.

Again, as mediators, you're privileged to good fun stories as captured herein and also, those of unhappy endings, this is such a case. The parties enjoyed a very amicable relationship, so each session was sound with the typical back and forth arguments to support their respective positions.

But these issues unknowingly at the time would be the last of the contract proposals to be negotiated. As the parties continued their recommendations, the Union countered with one that surely would move the contract closer to an agreement. It was to cleanse all employee's current attendance status. Those in the progressive discipline would move a step back. Which, at that time, would end the contract bargaining, with wages and health care resolved. The remaining open items accepted as per the last proposal recorded.

Then as the parties reconvened the next afternoon, heartbreak ensued! The employer was closing its operation! Nothing left to bargain except; "effects bargaining." (page 115) So, what the hell is that? It's bargaining on the closure of the plant; on items such as; severance pay, resume writing assistance, unemployment officers brought in to help the laid-off employees fill out those forms, etc. *A negotiation you never want to be involved in!*

So, the empty bag analogy. One day bargaining over wages, health care, attendance, etc., and then the next; outplacement negotiations. Why did I share this story as part of the book? Because it's necessary to understand the bargaining process and what can happen, the worst-case scenario was here in this case. **Sometimes there is nothing one can do, but always being aware and sharing such circumstances is a crucial part of life in contract bargaining.**

Lesson: Worst case scenario

CHAPTER TWENTY-SIX
Why not strike? Mediators lesson.

Here's another story from my mediation memory. An employer under a new C.E.O., Chief Executive Officer, decided to upgrade the facility. Remember, I mentioned the word "trust?" well, this is an excellent example of what a lack of trust can do. This particular Union membership committee, due to past poor experience with the previous C.E.O., would not believe that the upgrade was for the improvement of the company, but thought it was to sell the facility and that accordingly, all could lose their jobs.

So how do you develop trust? By keeping your word, remember. This C.E.O. was reaching out to the Union bargaining committee and membership, for "Trust." But the committee was fired up, and they were not in a trusting mood. But to force the issue and demand language that would cement their security. This commonly called "Job Security," language in contract bargaining. This particular committee was not a seasoned one, strong but lacking weathered experience of long-term bargainers.

The mediator, as part of his role, told a little story to help move the negotiations to a settlement. As the trust he had in discussions with the employer was that the action considered was just that; to improve the facility, keep it, and become competitive. A strike would have a reverse impact. Would have closed the facility, and the employees would have lost their employment.

So, the mediator's story went like this; "The first week of the strike, if paid weekly, the first week will have little or no impact on the members as they're going to receive a paycheck from the week before. But now you're in the 2nd and 3rd week with no money, household bills are adding up and now **you** members of the negotiating committee, askes the mediator to set another meeting. The mediator asks for another bargaining session, but here is what could happen. I ask to resume the negotiations. And the attorney for the employers says, "the owner is out of the country for a month!" They are not authorized to meet until the owners return! Oh! So, now the strike will be moving into its 7th week and still no date, as the owner's availability is not guaranteed.

Leverage!

Lesson: This could be an exceedingly actual scenario and is another reason to be prepared for the **"Worst case scenario."**

The parties eventually created a labor-management committee per the mediator's suggestion. The facility made improvements, along with its new working partnership with the union, accomplished at the right time!

Holy shit, they're on the street!?

Here's another mediation case that has some humor. I was assigned a situation in which a strike was imminent. Which was the first time that I met the parties. The meeting was on the 2nd floor of the FMCS (Federal Mediation & Conciliation Services) office building. The caucus rooms were no more than twenty-five feet away.

The bargaining session had been going on for about a month before I was assigned. So, the Union was taking a caucus to work on a counter proposal and said they would be ready in a little while. Part of a mediator's job is to communicate on the progress of negotiations when the parties are working separately. I told the management team to relax, and I would get back to them. I walked back into the Union caucus room, and the Union said there were going to lunch and would finish their proposal after lunch. I went back to inform the management team, of whom I just left about two minutes earlier. When I did, one manager was reading a book, another the newspaper, and yet another on eating a snack! I started laughing and said, damn when I said to relax your sure did. They all laughed. Then I suggest that they go to lunch also.

Now back with the parties, and the Union was telling me their proposal, "Verbally," e.g., you go tell management that we want them to stop f----ing around and get serious on the ----ing money! Again, this was the first time I had met with either party. So, I decided to deliver the message, but clean it up a little. As I entered the management caucus room and gave a, "cleaned up," Union proposal, one of the managers looked out the 2nd story window and exclaimed, "Hey there on the street, leaving! Ordered me to get them**! I replied," what the hell do you want me to do, "tackle them?"** The next meeting a couple of days later, I first met with the Union committee, who were all sitting, except the Union President. I said, "I'm not delivering any more messages until you sit down, as the last time you were all on the streets while I was giving your proposal. They all laughed, and within two more sessions, the parties reached and a handshake and eventual ratification.

John Gibson, January 2020 took the photo

SHORT STORY
Telework-saving the ----ing Whales!

So, another humorous case, yes, this is collective bargaining, believe it or not!

A lot of the public has heard about "Telework." And if you haven't, it's now part of collective bargaining agreements in and out of the collective bargaining world. A Federal Sector Union and the Agency are in a deadlock in negotiations on several issues. The stress of these issues put aside for the time being to handle a more straightforward problem in the contract, Telework/working remotely-at home. Good decision, right? What you are about ready to read will show you it wasn't easy.

The parties were going through the issue of (working at home) telework, to do specific tasks that could be performed outside of the four walls of the agency. Now there has to be a process set up to accomplish this and still have supervision involved.

Set of issues to allow telework;

1. An employee working from their home must be available for the supervisor to reach them about any updates or changes in assignments.
2. The employee has to be available for conference calls from supervision.
3. The work at home schedule has to be such as to have the employee available to return to the agency for face to face meetings, e.g., department meetings

4. The employee must communicate daily with his/her supervisor upon starting work at home. And upon completion of the day.
5. The home must meet Osha's safety standards.

So, after negotiating all of these successfully. The Union brought up the issue of giving each employee a phonecard; thus, they're not subject to any long-distance call at their own expense. The agency said, 'don't worry, the employees, ("ee's") will not have to make ANY long-distance calls, so no need for any phone card.

The Union persisted that they still felt the need for phone cards for the ee's working at home. Also, the Union suggested that Telework be allowed in ½ half days.

The agency replied, "full-day increments only, the agency cannot be worried about monitoring a workweek broken down as such. The Union sparred with, "give us phone cards." At this point, after several sessions of contract bargaining and feeling that to move things ahead with Telework ended up being a disaster. The Union, "We want phone cards period!" The agency at its wit's end, exploded, 'No ----ing cards, no ----ing ½ day telework, stop the ----ing asinine proposals and let's ----ing get back to serious ----ing negotiations do you ----ing understand and again NO ----ing ½ days too much gas! The Union replied, "gas? What? We're not here to save the ----ing Whales!!

At this point, this case is under the auspices of mediation, I could not help but end the heated conversation, with a question to the agency, "did I hear this right? Is the Agency not supplying phone cards?? Which was followed by a stare that would burn holes in lead. Only to realize that I had a smile and tears running down my face, a face as a mediator that should always be stoic. When another member of the management committee remarked, "you are enjoying this, aren't you?" I said, "I can't help it; no one would believe this; **I should write a book.** Then with laughter all around, the meeting ended, and in two more sessions, the parties reached agreement on a new Term Agreement.

I know sometimes you might talk about a specific circumstance and looking back, saying how funny it was. But believe me, this was funny then!

SHORT STORY
The Art of Communication

Here's another somewhat amusing story. A private-sector negotiation wherein the parties had been negotiating periodically over a month. The last two sessions under the auspices of a Mediator, again, me. Now, remember this is a private sector where the Union can strike the Employer. So, it's critically important to communicate from a mediator's standpoint most critical. During the negotiations, the mediator may visit each party during their caucus. And deliver proposals and counter-proposals that MUST be accurate. You can imagine that if a message was delivered by the mediator that was miscommunicated, the parties could, "Walkout," sessions over and tempers raised to the point that neither may want to resume bargaining!

It was now about 4 pm when the parties broke, and the Union said that they were going to take the employer's final proposal back to the members to either accept or take a strike vote! The Union had rented a hall in which to give the employees the employer's last proposal and ask for a vote. The Union leadership asked me to attend and provide members with a short statement. In mediation, attendance at Union ratification is not usually recommended. If you do attend your comment should be, "both parties worked hard." Period.

So, I did attend, made that statement, and gave the Business Agent my business card and asked to **call my Cell** after the meeting with the results. I left the ratification around 5 pm and headed home about a 40-minute trip. At home, I'm waiting for the call. It became 6:15 pm faster than usual. Then it was 7 pm? I'm wondering, "what the hell happened? Are they striking on the street?" I turn on the news, holding my breath. Now's it's 8 pm!!!

I was walking back and forth like I'm waiting for a daughter to come home on her first date! I couldn't' wait any longer, and out of desperation, at 8:30 pm, I called the Business Agents cell. Upon reaching the agent and explaining my anxiety, he said, *"Who in the hell gives someone their business card and tells them to call them on the cell **when the CELL number is NOT ON THE BUSINESS CARD!"** ☺ The contract was ratified overwhelmingly.

The Business card with **no cell.**

SHORT STORY
Risking a career

They're times, but very few and in-between that someone risks their career, for a higher goal. Especially if the risk is being taken in labor negotiations, and the result could be the loss of their position! The year was somewhere around 2005, and a sizeable federal sector Union and large federal Agency were in a "Blood Bath," setting of their most robust Term Bargaining. The sessions had gone on for months. Some 40 plus Articles were up for negotiations, and all but 12 resolved.

The Union was taking the entire package to the membership via mail-in ballot, a process that took a couple of months. After all the votes, the contract rejected! Now what? Agency was not in favor of the Union doing a recount, time, and expense. Remember, in the Federal Sector, a lot of Labor-Management negotiations are paid by the taxpayers.

During the last couple of weeks, the parties requested a mediator from the Federal Mediation and Conciliation Service to work with the parties. Yes, guess what, that mediator was me. The local Union committee was not in favor of the contract either, as the term, "Blood Bath," was what they called it. The Agency's position was, "if there is a recount, the final package will be worst!" Being a mediator that came from the private sector labor union, and being aware that some of those Unions, faced with such a dilemma, would accept the contract by the authority of the bargaining committee.

Unfortunately, this was not the private sector, and no such authority existed or used. Realizing this, I asked for the Top National Union President, who was the *prior local President, for this local* to step in and accept the contract on his authority. He did, and the following year almost lost his reelection as National President! A brave move and one that saved the membership despite their vote. A contract much better than a follow-up recount would have resulted in thanks to National union leader John Gage. **A Top Song that year 2005 was;** *We belong together...*so true.

Lesson: Knowledge.

SHORT STORY
An Earthquake

Here's another true story concerning collective bargaining. The parties are in the 3rd-week negotiations, and to put it mildly. The tempers are at a fever pitch. Once again, mediation from the FMCS was requested, and I was the mediator assigned. The negotiations continued on a relatively sunny day, great weather outside, and a stormy conversation inside. I took my place at the head of the bargaining table and was taking time to admire my cell phone update I just received. A BlackBerry, Classic.

It wasn't unusual for the parties during a hot subject to holler and banged the table with their fists. I guess I was just used to that type of meeting from when I was an advocate. It really didn't bother me, and I just let the parties go at it, get the steam off, as this particular day, I was more interested in checking out my cell. As the banging and hollering went on, it seemed that the whole damn table started to vibrate! I felt now it's time to split the parties to let them cool down. **When out of the corner of my eye, I saw a chair was moving across the room.** What!? It was an earthquake, and I'm thinking it was the parties banging on the table. When I looked up and they all looking at me, and all said at once," we're **having an Earthquake!** *The year 2007, a top song* **The Sweet Escape!** *And it was as we all left the building. Oh well, welcome to the world of collective bargaining.*

CHAPTER TWENTY-SEVEN
Can a Union be a positive influence?

Management and Union as one.

Currently, about 8% present of the American workforce is Union organized.

A remarkably low number considering the representation one can get for an initiation fee and a moderate level of dues.

For example, if an employee is charged with breaking a company rule or policy, and disciplined under a Union contract, the employee has;

1. A first-line representative/steward to consult with or to file a grievance on their behalf.

2. If no resolution, there is usually a higher-level representative or steward to try and resolve the issue through additional meetings with the respective supervisor.

3. If still no resolution, the usual grievance procedure has either 2-3 Grievance Steps (meetings with management) to get all the information/evidence in an attempt to resolve the issue in dispute.

4. If no resolution happens here, the grievance is usually now reviewed by still higher representatives (officers), including the Union Business Agent or Union President. Along with the review of its executive board or grievance committee.

5. At this point, some Unions after No. 4, have an attorney on retainer or an in-office attorney to review the issue and discuss

whether the issue/grievance has merit and whether or not it should go to arbitration.

6. Then depending on the contractual language in the grievance and arbitration sections and the specifics of the case. The issue can proceed to an arbitrator for a final and binding decision.

Of course, in the above structure, Weingarten Rights have already been applied.

All this protection and representation for the price of a monthly or weekly dues payment! Including the effort that goes into the term collective bargaining contract negotiation. Negotiations to gain in addition to wages; Cost of Living Adjustments (COLA), General Increases, other rights and protections for the members such as; sick days, vacation, seniority protection, severance packages, personal time off, a grievance procedure, job classifications, healthcare, pension, and 401k language.

Plus, the various lobbying efforts with the U.S. Congress or those at State and Local levels, to increase **benefits** for both labor and **management.**

Management? Oh yes, *lobbying efforts by Unions* (see Chapter 28 and 29) to help secure contracts for; Federal, State/Local levels, and Private employers. That helps gain additional work, "job security," thereby increasing your employment longevity.

Union Membership in the United States: *

1930 28% of wage earners
2010 12% of wage earners
2019 08%? of wage earners
*% are approximate.

CHAPTER TWENTY-EIGHT
The labor of Lobbying—Management & Labor as one

For a long time across the country, the feeling is that labor organizations are known only as being a disruptive force. Strikes are a hindrance to the company. But, I'm here to tell you there is an entirely different side and a very positive one. One that I was personally involved—the power of lobbying, lobbing for contracts that will not only strengthen the employer. But would add job security to the Union membership. There can be multiple employers making the same product. Some of these employers have no Union presence, others do. At the plant that I started to work, there were three Unions, as stated in an earlier chapter. I and the Union Presidents from the other two Unions got together, **not to bargain,** but **to lobby for contracts,** that our members could benefit. Not just for immediate employment, but future job security.
And in 1987 this is how it started

Meeting with U.S. Senator Paul Sarbanes, L-R IUE local 130 President Bob Reed, me, Senator Sarbanes, I.B.E.W. local 1805

President Gladys Greene, and Westinghouse lobbyist. A top song in 1987: **Nothing's Gonna Stop Us Now.**

And nothing did. Followed by this inspiring letter on the next page from President Reagan to the three Unions for the efforts and solidarity.

January 16, 1987

Dear Mr. Eder:

I want to take this opportunity to thank you for your
efforts in support of my Fiscal Year 1987 defense budget.
My Administration is proud to have had the support of all
three labor unions at Westinghouse during last year's
debate over America's national security needs. Although we
didn't get everything we wanted, I'm deeply grateful for
your show of solidarity.

We've made tremendous progress in the last six years in
rebuilding our military strength. We've worked to make
sure that those defending our freedom have the weapons
and equipment they need and deserve. And here in
Washington the members of my Administration never lose
sight of what has made this progress possible: the support
and activities of people like you. We couldn't have done it
without you.

As you know, however, there's a lot more that remains to
be accomplished. Already, the battle for the 1988 budget
is shaping up in the Congress. With your help, we will
succeed in our drive to insure that America's Armed
Forces, the world's vanguard in defense of liberty, are
second to none. I hope I can continue to count on your
invaluable support in the coming year.

Again, my thanks for everything you have already done.
God bless you.

Sincerely,

Ronald Reagan

99

And, even with a change in the leadership of the I.U.E. local 130. The three Union Presidents continued to lobby for contracts for the benefit of the employer and our members. Here above, <u>meeting with U.S. Senator Joe Lieberman on Defense programs. From L-R, Myself (S.E.A.) Senator Lieberman, Gladys Greene (IBEW -1805) and Rick O'Leary (IUE -130 Now 1988, a top song was "Roll with it." And we did!</u>

We also later worked with and through a Washington DC lobbyist, Michael Balzano of Balzano and Associates. A man who later became our friend and supporter. Though these efforts, we were able to gain essential programs. Programs that not only supplied additional work for all of our memberships but also increase hiring opportunities, opportunities that increased our respective bargaining units.

The employers' Motto was; "Error Free Performance **2nd to None.**" And we weren't. We started to beat the competition and beat them regularly. Getting awarded contracts that our collective memberships, along with the companies engineering, program, and managerial staff, worked hard to produce, making the motto a real one. These lobbying efforts included the Union leaderships requesting and getting our members to fill out Thousands of Hand Written letters addressed to their respective congressional representatives, that the Union leadership, (hand-carried and delivered to those representatives in person.)

This, as you can imagine, had an overwhelmingly positive impact. In the next chapter, you'll see evidence of these actions. As via the lobbyist contacts, we created an even more influential group of Unions expanding from the West Coast to the East Coast. Our lobbyist Mike Balzano christened the group the; National Aerospace Workforce Coalition, later to be called the National Workforce Coalition.

CHAPTER TWENTY-NINE
The National Aerospace Workforce Coalition

Throughout this chapter, I will demonstrate the various lobbying efforts that resulted in success. A success that not only helped our collective memberships but helped our employer, a Win-Win, situation. I put these two chapters in my book to demonstrate the importance of working together for a common goal. And to show what a positive influence a Union organization can have.

This organization that was created around 1986, and guess what the **Top Song was; "That's What Friends are For."** These **Friends** comprised this coalition of leaderships from; my Union the Salaried Employees Association, the (I.B.E.W.) International Brotherhood of Electrical Workers, Local 1805, the (I.U.E.) the International Union of Electricians local 130 from Maryland, the (A.L.P.A.), American Airlines Pilots Association, the (I.A.M.) International Association of Machinists from St. Louis, MO, the Association of Scientists and Professional Personnel (A.S.P.E.P.), from New Jersey, the Southern California Professional Engineering Association (S.C.P.E.A.), the Council of Engineers and Scientists Organization (C.E.S.O.) from California and (S.P.E.E.A.), Society of Professional Engineering Employees from Seattle, Washington and others. Here in the next couple of pages are photos of the coalition's efforts.

The National Aerospace Coalition members below meeting with Secretary of Defense Richard Cheney and California Governor Pete Wilson, in support of programs for our employers and our members, Governor Wilson 2nd from left and Secretary of Defense Richard Cheney 7th from left.

Coalition members meet with U.S. Senator Sam Nunn, Chairman of Senate Arms Services Committee, in Georgia, for Christening of the B2 Bomber, of which our members made the radars. I believe the initial order for B2 was 50 one for each state, but due to budget constraints, only 20 were made.

President Clinton meeting with Westinghouse Electric, Defense Center President Dick Linder, 2nd from left, I.B.E.W. President Gladys Greene obscured by the President, myself, and I.U.E. President Rick O'Leary. President Clinton visited Westinghouse to review Aerospace programs that were in production and on schedule.

1997 a top hit, I Believe I can fly.

National Aerospace Workforce Coalition is meeting In 1992 with President George H.W. Bush. At the end of his term. (The President seated his with back to camera 2nd from left) on the Defense budget and contracts for our employers, and our members.

A top song that year, " Just Another Day." It was for us, as I'm sure it was for the President!

National Workforce Coalition meeting the Senators Ashcroft and Santorum. In support of programs for our respective employers/ employees and members. Senator Ashcroft is 2nd from left, and Senator Santorum is 2nd from the right.

This picture taken in 1988, I had left National contract bargaining in Pittsburgh, Pa, to fly to New Orleans to speak to R.N.C. platform committees on behalf of the Defense Budget and met with President H.W. Bush just after his speech addressing the convention.

The top song that year, "Faith."

"AUTHOR DEFINITIONS"

IF YOU want to reach agreements, it's also imperative to develop a reputation as one who can be trusted, and you can do that through one on one conversations, and keeping that conversation **one *on one!*** It' an excellent method of creating that trusting relationship. That's so very important in the labor-management world or any part of your life. ***Think about it,*** **when you have a one on one conversation, and it *stays one on one* that's the definition of Trust.**

Hey, and guess what, that is a two-way street. It is telling a confidential comment/situation to the opposing counterpart and vice versa. The most important part of this. Is keeping it secret until the agreed-upon time to disclose is agreed.

One on One: A conversation between two persons to be kept confidential between those two persons and no one else! Not your best friend, not even your pillow, NO ONE ELSE! It's a development of trust and confidence in you.

***An Off the record* discussion**; is a discussion either between two persons or in a group setting. That cannot be referred back to or used in another situation. A conversation to reach out on a "what if situation." To explore issues or opportunities that are not on the record.

Bargaining notes: During contract negotiations, each party may take minutes/notes of the proceeding. If both parties **agree** and share the notes after each session, then they can be part of the record of negotiations. Sometimes the parties will use one **mutually agreed** to note-taker and may have another one to alternate. These so-called; bargaining meeting minutes, negotiation minutes, or bargaining notes that are part of the negotiations.

But, (there is that word again) if there is no such agreement then any separate notes that are taken are just that, separate and are only suitable for a wood-burning fireplace☹

CHAPTER THIRTY
Collective Bargaining Definitions

Bargaining committee; consists of members that are selected or elected to serve during contract bargaining. They are separate committees for the leadership of management and the Union. The committees after the negotiation are complete, usually prepare a synopsis of the contract. This synopsis has highlights to bring back for ratification of the members and acceptance of the; Owner, C.E.O., if Private Sector, The Mayor, or City/County Counsel if State or County If Public Sector and the agencies Commissioner; Agency Head Review, if Federal Sector.

Caucus: A recess or break in negotiations, requested by the party that wants to discuss issues of bargaining separately. These caucuses are private, and the information discussed can be shared or kept private.

Quid Pro Quo; the *give and take* in negotiations. Something one gives up to receive something in equal weight. And the Equal weight of the exchange is determined by each party.

M.O.U., Memorandum of Understanding; a negotiated written document to create an understanding in writing that is not currently in the C.B.A.

An M.O.A., Memorandum of Agreement; also, a negotiated written document to create an agreement in writing that is not currently in the C.B.A.

An Addendum is a separate attachment to a C.B.A. It is usually listed/titled at the end of the contractual language of the C.B.A.

The A. F. L.-C. I. O. (American Federation of Labor and the Congress of Industrial Organizations) was founded in 1955. The A.F.L-C.I.O Is the "Mother" of labor organizations and is the largest union organization in the U.S.A. It is comprised of Federal, State, and Local and Private sector unions, known as affiliates such as U.A.W., U.M.W., U.S.W.A., A.L.P.A., N.F.L.P.A., M.L.B.P.A., A.F.G.E., N.T.E.U., A.F.S.C.M.E. and many more.

Affiliates; a group of unions organized, usually under one master agreement but with various employers. Each (affiliate-local) bargains independently on issues relevant to the employees represented. With typically the economics negotiated under the master agreement.

Local; a union representing employees at usually a singular employer but can have contracts with other unrelated employers. A local can be independent or part of a group of affiliates under one large Union and a national organization

The "Change to Win Federation; organization created 2005 represents, State/Local and private sector unions and has two previously independent unions the; (I.B.T.) International Brotherhood of Teamsters, (S.E.I.U.) Service Employees International Union are now this organization's member. This organization is an alternative to the AFL-CIO national organization.

Independent unions; These are unions not affiliated with the AFL-CIO or not under a National Union organization. The (F.I.S.U.) Federation of Independent Salaried Unions is an independent union.

C.B.A.; Collective Bargaining Agreement, is a signed document memorializing the agreed to language that forms a contract.

Job classification/descriptions; A list of job duties or responsibilities that are incorporated usually in a one to two-page paper. The listing of Primary/critical functions, routine responsibilities, education, experience, in the department, and across department responsibilities. These classification or job descriptions usually are assigned a pay level with associated job level numbers, e.g., 12-14-16, etc. a level 12 would have specific duties, and a level 14 successfully higher responsibilities and a level 16 yet higher. Each with corresponding pay increases.

A Progressions/ladders; These are a listing of job classifications/descriptions in ascending orders, e.g., 12-14-16. Progressions would have similar titles; Planning, Purchasing, Engineering, Accounting, Technical Services, Sale Clerk, Sales Associate, Sales Leader, etc. These progressions or "ladders" are set up for employees to progress within their field of skills. Such as Planner III to Planner II to Senior Planner, etc. So, based on skills could advance up the "ladder."

Bargain in Good Faith; "Handled under the N.L.R.A. and F.L.R.A." I just wanted to expand on this from the U.L.P. reference above. Bargaining in good faith means; The parties must agree to meet and confer at reasonable times and locations over issues that are required by law and or contract; C.B.A. For example, when parties are in the same geographical area (both in Maryland), One party cannot agree to meet only in a location, say South West Texas. Or only agree to only meet outside regular business hours. Like at 3 am to 4 am to impose a bargaining obstacle/hardship to the other party.

D.F.R.; Duty of fair representation; This is a complaint filed with the N.L.R.B. or F.L.R.A. by an employee in a labor organization, charging the Union with a failure to represent employees equally. This type of charge claiming an employee treated differently than other employees in the bargaining unit.

C.B.C.; Coordinated Bargaining Committee, different Unions collectively bargaining together, wherein they have memberships at the same employer. A bargaining strategy used to gain leverage in the negotiations.

Ratification is the process that happens after contract bargaining. The respective memberships can vote on either rejection or acceptance of the newly negotiated contract. If accepted its, "Ratified,"

Term bargaining; the major contract negotiation usually separated by the number of months, years between contract negotiations. The term could be three years, I years or a continuing time until one party requests to open, "bargaining."

Mid-Term bargaining is the bargaining **(during)** while the contract term is ongoing, between the beginning date and expiration date.

Mid-Term modification; This a requested change to the language of the current language of the existing C.B.A. During the term between the ratification and termination. In the private sector, unless desirable, the parties don't have to bargain and cannot be forced into a mandatory bargaining scenario. But be careful, once entertaining the suggested language modification, the parties could give up its ability to oppose the language.

Impasse: During a negotiation, when the parties reach a point when they have no more movement to offer and seem to be in a stalemate, it called an impasse.

Bargaining Chip: An item one party has that another party may want or need. So it can be traded or another item during bargaining.

Effects Bargaining is when an employer decides to close its operation. As a result, no more bargaining occurs. Except for the negotiation over the outplacement of the employees on such subjects as; resume preparation, severance pay, unemployment insurance claim assistance, health insurance availability, for the laid-off/terminated employees. Plus, setting up any career counseling or current and future job fairs or opportunities. See Chapter twenty-five, "The Empty Bag," this the most detrimental time in negotiations. The situation sometimes happens; after bargaining on benefits and enhanced contract, language is over. And, for whatever business reason, an employer closes its operation.

Severance pay; Sometimes, in a labor agreement, "C.B.A." There is language incorporated that in the event of a plant closure or move, employees based on years of service will receive a contractually agreed amount of money for each year of seniority/service. In some instances, even with no such previously negotiated language, an employer may offer some financial assistance.

O.S.H.A.: Occupational Safety and Health Administration; A government agency set in place to monitor safe and healthy working conditions at employers, agencies, facilities, either on a route teen basis or by request.

M.O.S.H.A.: Maryland Occupational Safety and Health Administration; A State agency to accurately monitor State employers concerning safe and healthy practices in the workplace. It can routinely monitor or be requested by the employer or employee.

A Side-Letter, a document written to capture an agreement, usually negotiated during the term of the agreement, sometimes included in the C.B.A. or if not, **should be** recorded in both the H.R. and Union office files.

A Supplement can be one or a series of supplemental contractual written documents; to supplement language the Master Agreement, usually listed in the C.B.A. by title/reference.

A Covered Item: is a language already existing in a C.B.A., e.g., in a grievance procedure, harassment, which is a covered item that can be grieved.

CHAPTER THIRTY-ONE
The Act's

N.L.R.A.; **National Labor Relations Act**, this is the Private sector law on union elections, unfair labor practices of both employers and unions, D.F.R.'s, employee rights, to join a union or to refuse to join a union, labor, and management responsibilities. It disseminates its procedures via the **N.L.R.B.,** National Labor Relations Board. The N.L.R.A. created in 1935, then called the Wagner Act. Amended in 1947 as the Taft-Hartley Act. Culminating after that as the N.L.R.A.

Under the **N.L.R.A.** The agency for dispute resolution and conflict management provides mediation services to Private, Public, and Federal Sector employers and unions.

FMCS; Federal Mediation & Conciliation Service, A Federal agency established in 1947.

F.L.R.A.; Federal labor relations Authority established in 1978. Which is the Federal Sector law on union-management relations. (Sometimes called the "Sister," labor law to the NRLA.) U.L.P.'s employee rights, management and Union rights, D.F.R.'s, Unfair labor practices filed by an agency, or a union resolved under this act, which was

F.S.I.P.; Federal Services Impasse Panel, Federal statute agency established under the F.L.R.A., that hears Federal Sector labor/management impasses and makes the final, binding decisions with an order issued.

U.L.P. Unfair Labor Practice; is a complaint or charge against either the union or the employer, refusing to bargain in good faith. It can be initiated by either party. U.L.P.'s are addressed/resolved by the **N.L.R.B. or F.L.R.A.** for Private and Federal sectors, respectively.

WEINGARTEN ACT

Weingarten Act; a Supreme court decision of 1975, that give employees the right to request a representative or another party to attend a meeting called by the employer, if the employee feels the subject of the meeting could result in disciplinary action against the employee. So, if you're that employee going to a meeting that you may feel like a disciplinary action could ensue, make sure *you ask for a representative,* **"Before the next teardrop falls."** A top hit that year!

Weingarten Rights

1. The employee must request that a Union representative be present.
2. The employee must have a reasonable belief that discipline may result from questioning.
3. The employee. is entitled to get information for the employer about the subject of the meeting/questioning.
4. The employee is entitled to consult with his/her Union representative in private.
5. Union representative is entitled to consult with the employee in private.
6. The employer has the right to stop the questioning of the employee.
7. The employee is not entitled to Union representation. If the employer is only informing the employee of some discipline that has already been decided.

8. The employee has no right to refuse to attend meetings with the employer if Union representation is not provided.

9. The employee does not have the right to a Union representative of his/her choice; Union representation may be based on the availability of a Steward/Representative.

AFTERWORD

One never knows what the future will hold for them. Either in longevity, genes, (inherited skills) developed skills, career opportunities, wealth, poverty, and health. Indeed, I didn't. Especially as I walked to school following my first failed negotiations with my mother. After failing so miserably at that, a future in negotiations was laughable at best.

All of us, I think, are either driven in a direction by outside influences, influences that they're not even aware of the impact at that time, you can fall onto a course, like it, and then go into a different direction. Whatever it may be, make sure when you discover it, take hold and cherish it.

As I said at the outset of this writing, I always felt the need to assist someone, help a person in need. Share something of value, perceived or real, rejoice in the results. I used to say I started delivering the WALL STREET JOURNAL as a mail clerk and progressed to the position where instead of just distributing, I was now reading it. Not smart enough to digest its readings, but intelligent enough, I believe, to realize the accomplishment.

Hopefully, one part of this book will put not only help from the standpoint of saving some, ($$$) in your day to day life of negotiations. Assist you in your role as a negotiator in contract bargaining, either of which would be great. But also to open a road that you can excel in and then share it with someone else.

IN CLOSING

As I close this book, I also want to thank some other people that stood by me and had a positive influence on me in every phase of my employment.

*Starting with, U.S. Navy, It was 1st Class Vincent Bonadio who used his influence during a tropical storm at sea. Keeping me from climbing onto the forward gun mount to re-attach a 20-foot wiping radio antenna in 25-30-mile winds while the ship was heaving to and fro. An order that, if carried out, could have most possibly ended my existence.

* Westinghouse/Northrup Grumman/employment, Aunt Thelma, who got me the job. My friends from the printed circuit board planning group; Stan Rataczyck, Wayne Loyd, Robert Luipaeter, and Loran Estell. Also, Mike Grimes, Larry Cline, Ray Burke, Joe Halley, Al Gordon, Jim Fitzgerald, Dan Bruno, John Maur, Ralph Crabill, Warren Wilkie, Charol Chelton, and the supervisor previously mentioned Ray Stull. Also, some fantastic ladies; Margaret Kratz-Amland, Patricia Hands, Ginny Swain. Carol Louden, Paulet Boswell, Suzy Gardner, Margie Quinn, Jeannie Warfield, Penny Upton, Donna Ziegenhein, and Sharon Pearl.

*As a President of the Salaried Employee Union, Julia Hafner, John Chilcote, Beth Varner, Bill Ziegenhein, Don Strawser, Karl Tucker, Howard Hergenhan, Bruce Lascola, Bud Schmidt, Ron Hoffman, Denny Wilderson, Bob Wagner, Joe Alt, Joe Hiltz, Mike Pearl, John Custer,

Ken Wholey, Jeff Grant, Don Scannell, Rick Griffith, Ray Williams, Don Schrader, Ike Johnson, Jim Johnson, Jim McCartney, Rodem Nelson, Vince Ellsworth, Culis Glenn, Jack Schuler, Don Schrader, Bob Gardner, and Frank Miller. Plus, all the members that voted for me each election from 1972 until 2000, enabling me to reach the position I'm in today.

*As a Vice President of the Federation of Independent Salaried Unions, Ira Matthews, Damian Testa, Rich Mori, Patrick Thomassey, Dan Gavin, Mike Bodinski, and all the affiliate officers that voted for me as Vice President.

*Other positive influences; Other positive influences; Baltimore City Labor Commissioner Debra Moore Carter and Office Mgr. Lavetta Webster, N.L.R.B. region 5 past Chairs; Wayne Gold & Louie D'Amico, City Union of Baltimore, Ruth Pajuhandi, Thaddeus Goode & James Anthony, Baltimore City Fire Fighters and Officers past Presidents; Mike Campbell, & Steve Fugate, I.B.T. local 570 President Rich Brown and Sean Cedenio', M.L.E.A. Officers; Mary Landry, Don Kellner, Al Lloyd, and Ed Pedrick. Gamse Lithographic; Plant Mgr., Mark Ledonne and Sue Pace U.S.W.A. local President, William T Burnett & Co., Inc; Plant Mgr. Ken Gower & Don Harris Local I.U.E. Pres., Abato Rubinstein & Abato, Jim Rosenberg & Vickie Hedian, Shaw and Rosenthal, Michael McGuire & Art Brewer, IBT 355 President Denis Taylor, Vulcan Hart; Hr Director, Fleming Scott, and Executives, Darin Furguson, Chris Bauermann, and Brian Fosse, & Boilermaker past Presidents of local lodge 193 Wilton Barnett & Alex Poling. Amports; Plant Mgr., George Molyneaux & IBT 335 rep., Jim Deene. Training Director Aberdeen, Frank Roig, LaFarge Holcim Cement Co. Steve Heagy and John Lewis U.S.W.A. local 33 Presidents., Kahn Smith & Collins, F J Collins. and U.F.C.W. Buddy Mays prior local President.

*Management influences; Westinghouse/Northrup Grumman: Richard Linder, Ed Silcott, Aris Melissaratos, Vic Deltuva, Bud Wyble, Pete Bishop, Bill Gore, Bob Barnes, Neil Burns, Mike Jackson, Barnett Brooks, Ron Suski, Jack Thompson, John Spuirrier, Ron Rattell, Bob Treude, George Citroni, Gordon Citroni, and Cam Watt.

*Influences as a Commissioner of Mediation; From, John Calhoun Wells, Ken Kowalski, Richard Barnes, D. Scott Blake, Bill Carlisle, John Pinto, Scot Beckenbaugh, George Cohen, Alison Beck. To Walt Bednarczyk, Larry Passwaters, Harry Aikens, Sharon Rafferty, Donna Filosa, Pete Donatello, Fran Leonard, Bill McFadden, Dan LeClair, Mike Wolf, Andrew Long, Karen Kline, Barbara Lichtman, Randy Mayhew, Christy Yoshitomi, Shakima Wright, Denise McKenney, Vanessa Bullock, Doug & Tony Jones, Heather Brown, Joe Schimansky, Damian Testa, Gary Kummell, Adam Ramsey, Arthur Pearlstein, Debra Moore Carter, Cet Parks, Byron Charlton, Richard Barchiesi, Terry Stapleton, and Bill Luyre, George Gaye and the FMCS class of 2000. Also, the entire FMCS office personal that supports the field mediators. They make everything happen.

*Arbitration; D. Scott Blake, William Lowe, David Vaughn, Ernie DuBester, Jim Strong, Fleming Scott, Witold Skwierczynski, Ralph Patinella, Ken Gower, John Livingood, and Walt De Treux

SPECIAL ACKNOWLEDGEMENTS

To the following, I owe my gratitude and appreciation. The support each gave in writing this book was invaluable, as is the love they provide continuously.

Karen Eder: my wife, best friend. She has always been there, supporting me, even in some of the darkest periods. To consistently bring light, with loving affection.

Julie Ann-Marie Grove: daughter and Senior editor. Always a smile and a loving heart. She and her husband David have blessed us with three beautiful grandchildren; Ella, Evelyn, and Ethan.

Melanie Joy Pizzini: daughter, entrepreneur, and editor. Always, with advice and loving hugs. She and her husband Larry also blessed us with three beautiful grandchildren; Logan, Gloria, and Landon.

Roy: my son, an entrepreneur. He also started employment as a labor grade two mail clerk, now a Director at a national beer distributor. He and his wife Lisa have blessed us with two beautiful grandchildren; Roy III and Eva.

William Eder: my older and richer brother and one to look up to in his work ethics and Christian beliefs. You couldn't have a more reliable person on your side. Always there to answer the most challenging question, a confidant.

Timothy Eder: my younger and other richer brother and now an established illustrator with three published books and working on one more. Always with a kind word for everyone and good thoughts, carried through in his strong Christian beliefs.

IN RECOGNITION

Donald Scott Blake: A current Director of Field Services for the Federal Mediation & Conciliation Service. And my previous manager. I appreciated his inspiration for always being there from the beginning as a mediator through and into arbitration.

Andrew Long III Esq: a long-time friend and personal attorney, who advised me to seek mediation. A confidant, one-time adversary, in which we developed an excellent personal relationship. A relationship of mutual respect during very stressful times that we were able to turn into fun experiences.

Damian Testa: A past National Union President of the National Federation of Independent Salaried Unions, (N.F.I.S.U.). And long-time friend. He could make even the most stressful bargaining, a fun time. I always needed to aware of a surprise joke.

Rich Giacolone: Will be the FIRST "out of the ranks" (FMCS)-Federal Mediation and Conciliation Service, Director when confirmed. A well-deserved appointment. Proud to have been a colleague of his, before my retirement from FMCS.

John Gage: Past President of America's largest Federal Sector Union, (A.F.G.E.) the American Federation of Government Employees. Currently, a labor consultant. A friend that, upon meeting for the first time, knew it would be a lifetime of trust.

Ralph Patinella: Past Associate Commissioner for the Office of Labor, Management, and Employee Relations for the Social Security Agency. Currently, an advisor to S.S.A. Another friend where "one on one" conversations were rock solid, just like him.

Doug Watley: Currently Social Security Administration's Chief Spokesperson for term negotiations. A man with a unique talent to be able to ease the tensions of bargaining, with his southern tone.

Jim Strong: Current Deputy Sub-Director for the United Steel Workers of America (U.S.W.A.). A long-time friend and almost a fellow Union officer with a potential USWA-SEA merger in the late '80s. A robust labor advocate.

Dr. Mike Balzano, Ph.D.: A friend and lobbyist involved in politics since the Nixon Presidency. And every administration since. A mentor for me in the political arena and close friend outside the political arena. He has written books to commemorate his efforts and his personal life experiences in, Building a New Majority, and his latest book Dyslexic (My journey).

James J. Kelley, Esq, Jim was an opponent in contract negotiations, during my tenure as a labor advocate and the unions chief lead negotiator. We developed a relationship of mutual respect. I appreciated the February 09, 2000 letter of congratulations upon my entering into the Federal Mediation & Conciliation Service.

Dion Guthrie: The longest-running local private sector Union president for the I.B.E.W. Local 1501. Strong labor advocate and a friend of **only** about 35 or so years.

Dr. Regional Wells, Ph.D.: A past Deputy Commissioner for the Office of Labor, Management, and Employee relations at S.S.A. and a current friend. He took the lead in assembling and sponsoring for S.S.A. an FMCS course on relationship building. A man of character and personal grace.

Bill Barry: A professor and former Director of a College Labor Studies Program. When you think you've experienced it all in the world of collective bargaining----then talk to Bill.

George Cohen, Esq: Past FMCS Director who brought to the agency, the positive and higher level of recognition it so well deserved. Working for him was a real pleasure.

Ernie Grecco: Past President of the Metropolitan Baltimore Council of the AFL-CIO. Our friendship dates back before 1985, a man of confidence and wisdom, respected by both the labor and management communities.

Bill McFadden: FMCS Commissioner, 1ST partner in FMCS...made my arrival in mediation so easy since he had everything up and running; all training programs, contacts, and office processes. I Appreciated his friendship and wit. I enjoyed working with him.

Milt Beever: Prior Deputy Commissioner for the Office of Labor, Management, and Employee Relations for Social Security Administration. A man of strong convictions and vision for S.S.A. A prior lead negotiator for S.S.A. in its contract with the forty-five thousand members A.F.G.E. Proud to call him a friend.

Michael Jackson: Westinghouse/Northrup Grumman HR Manager, although adversaries by positions held, developed a strong friendship during almost weekly meetings to address Union and Company issues. The kind of relationship that is so critical in the Labor-Management arena.

Scot Beckenbaugh: A past FMCS acting director during various administrations, shows his acceptance and worth. I Always enjoyed being in his company and under his "streetwise," leadership.

Julia Hafner: Past Union Executive board member who succeeded me as President, a dear friend, and confidant. A person of personal support and wisdom. The first woman Union President, as a matter of fact, the first woman, in each executive board position from my past local.

Larry Passwaters: FMCS Commissioner, became my best friend after Johns's passing. A confidant with strong feelings for family and friends.

Tom Funciello: Prior Associate Commissioner of the Office of Labor, Management, and Employee Relations for S.S.A. Although, worked with for a brief period, developed a friendship of trust.

Mike Bodinski: National Federation of Independent Salaried Unions, (N.F.I.S.U.) attorney and friend, solid with advice and friendship. Currently, lead general counsel for (O.P.E.I.U.) Office of Professional Employees International Union.

Patrick Thomassey: National Federation of Independent Salaried Unions counsel, long-time adviser, now in his private practice. An excellent person to have your back from a legal standpoint. We built a friendship through representing members.

Beth Varner: I nicked named "4.O," as she had that G.P.A. in college, Secretary-Treasurer of the Union and friend.

Karl Tucker: A Union Executive Board representative. A friend and magician with the computer. He was ahead of his time in that respect.

Bill Ziegenhein: Union Executive Board representative, always available to take on an impossible task. Long-time friend.

Witold Skwierczinsk: A Federal labor union advocate and influential leader, representing over 45 thousand employees as the chief spokesperson, had strong convictions and never-ending desire to fight for the members.

Denise Mckenney: FMCS Commissioner and the agencies EEO Director, her skills for the development of training materials are unmatched. A friend from the beginning.

Samuel "Sammy" Welsh: An initial mentor for me as a young labor advocate. Not sure if Sammy is still with us, but I know he would be proud.

Gary Kummel: A friend, began his career as a labor advocate, and ultimately became a Human Resource Manager, with whom I had the pleasure of negotiating with as adversaries. He made every business and personal meeting a fun experience.

Culis Glenn: Chief Steward and Executive Board member I.B.E.W. local 1805. A man of wit and common sense. During one of our many conversations on representation service for our members. He quoted, "We couldn't represent our members any better unless we handed out pillows as they entered the workplace."

AFL-CIO & Washington News Paper Guild: For the bargaining team for the AF of L; Richard Barchiesi, Terry Stapleton and Bill Luyre; for the Guild; Cet Parks and Byron Charlton. Probably the most stressful mediation of my career, but thanks to those listed, not only a successful outcome but a solid relationship built.

Walt Bednarczyk: FMCS Commissioner and my mentor. We developed an immediate and long-term friendship. His excellence in technology is unsurpassed. When met with any technological challenge that would make most panic, he addressed it with, "that's interesting." Then he corrects it.

ACKNOWLEDGMENTS (IN REMEMBRANCE)

Thelma Garretson: my Aunt, the youngest of my father's 5 five sisters, she got me the job at Westinghouse. With red hair and bright blue eyes, it was, however, her loving personality that stood out; God Bless her.

Gordan Swanson: Another long-time friend and staunch supporter during my advocate days. He affectionately called "The Six Million Dollar Man," as he had only 25% percent of Heart function. Not only could he take the ball on the run with it, but deliver it on time. Gone but never forgotten.

Howard Hergenhan: Union Executive Board representative and a close friend, with wisdom on how to brighten your day with such quips as: "It's a Rat Race and the Rats, are winning and "If I was feeling any better I have to take something for it." Left us at a very young age.

Karen Kline: A FMCS colleague, lovely, helping, kind, a person of value, and every other right word of goodness, one could think. She deserved them all.

Rich Mori: Prior National President of the Federation of Independent Salaried Unions, took over leadership in the early 1980s. He Chaired successive National contract negotiations through the 1980s into the early 1990s. And will be remembered as a President with an unexcitable personality and calming demeanor.

John Chilcote: A Union Executive Vice President. And before his passing, my best friend. I always referred to him as emulating the "Rock of Gibraltar," for he did. Will be continually remembered and missed.

Lee Nutt, Esq: Labor law professor, made each class fun, enjoyable, and entertaining from the start to the end, remembering him for his wit and sense of humor.

Jack Caspillera: Longtime U.S.W.A. officer and M.L.E.A. Sect./Treas. A man of wit and compassion, with a collective bargaining history that predates most.

ACKNOWLEDGMENTS (IN REMEMBRANCE.)

Thomas E. O'Leary: Former National Federation President late 1960's thru the mid-1970s. He initiated the first officer and representative manual that was used throughout his tenure and beyond. His famous quote, " Arbitrate & Negotiate, don't Aggravate & Eliminate.' Although we never met face to face, I realized he was a man of vision.

Raymond Stull: A Manager, my boss, and mentor who showed pride in my movement through the Union ranks. With a remembered quote, "Dress for the job you want, not for the job you have." A remark I took literally

Wil Schuerholz: Was the first (S.S.A.) Social Security Administrations, Director of Negotiations, and Litigations who I had the pleasurable learning experience. A man of strong convictions and assistance to others.

Donald Strawser: A Union Administrative Vice President. A friend and solid supporter throughout my Union career. Once saved me from being hit by a hanging metal anchor returning from a fishing trip! Don recently passed during this writing.

Gladys Greene: President and Business Manager of I.B.E.W. Local 1805, was not only a colleague in negotiations but a true friend for many years beyond.

Brenda Clayburn: President and Business Manager of C.U.B. Local 800. Developed this professional relationship via my role as Commissioner of Mediation. President Claburn was a true labor advocate with strong convictions and the strength to see them to completion.

I'm positive that after over 50 years of employment, I undoubtedly left people off this acknowledgment! My apologies for those. Not intentional but comes with age. ☺

As you can readily see, it takes colleagues, supervisors, union leaders and management leaders, friends, and, most of all, support and inspiration of your family. To advance in life, but most importantly, the Good Lord!

THANK YOU FOR READING THIS BOOK!

AUTHOR BIO

Gary L. Eder was born in Baltimore City, Maryland, on the morning of Sunday, June 8th, 1947, at 5: 57a.m of loving parents, William and Gloria Eder. Where growing up in the town of Glen Burnie, Maryland, he enjoyed a happy childhood. Upon graduation from high school in 1965, at age 18, he remembered looking at a calendar and thinking about retirement at 65, 2012! It seemed like an impossibility. Looked like a hill that he would never climb. But in 1965, with the Vietnam war in full swing, he enlisted in the U.S. Navy and started active duty in 1966, receiving an Honorable Discharge in 1972.

Upon his return, he took college evening classes where he excelled at 3.80 G.P.A., taking only specific collective bargaining, labor law, grievance handling, and labor studies related courses. Although he didn't know it then, it was the work experience and the specific college courses that ultimately allowed him to move to the position he's at today, just 27 summers later. Since that time, he has written several children's books; a series if you will; Uncle Wrigley and The Snow Bush, "A Christmas Story," Uncle Wrigley and Twigley the Flying Squirrels Candy and Cupcake Store, and Uncle Wrigley visits the Easter Bunny. He's written another children's book, now in the illustration phase, called Wigley, the Talking Fish.

Now in 2020, his employment spanning 53 plus years and continuing in his current position as a Labor Arbitrator/Mediator. He is currently living with his wife Karen in the resort area of Rehoboth Beach, Delaware, where he enjoys a successful arbitration practice while writing books. In this work, he hopes to share some skills in the art of negotiation. As an author, Gary's writings are wide-ranging, as, in addition to several children's books, he is currently writing a murder mystery novel; entitled 21 DAYS.

So from a part-time job at the Dairy Queen chain to Labor Arbitrator and Author. Guess what!

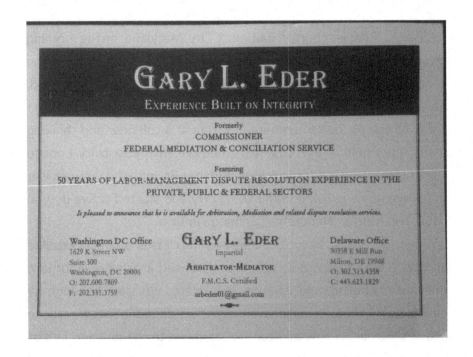

.....I can still make the curl on top of the Ice Cream cone☺

Seated in his home office with a smile. Thinking about the fun you'll have after reading this book. While he is thinking about his next book?

Printed in the United States
By Bookmasters